D1154715

AMERICAN EDUCATION

Its Men

Ideas

and

Institutions

Advisory Editor

The Rise of Local School Supervision in Massachusetts

Henry Suzzallo

ARNO PRESS & THE NEW YORK TIMES
*New York * 1969*

Reprint edition 1969 by Arno Press, Inc.

*

Library of Congress Catalog Card No. 70-89241

*

Reprinted from a copy in Teachers College Library

*

Manufactured in the United States of America

Editorial Note

AMERICAN EDUCATION: *Its Men, Institutions and Ideas* presents selected works of thought and scholarship that have long been out of print or otherwise unavailable. Inevitably, such works will include particular ideas and doctrines that have been outmoded or superseded by more recent research. Nevertheless, all retain their place in the literature, having influenced educational thought and practice in their own time and having provided the basis for subsequent scholarship.

Lawrence A. Cremin
Teachers College

The Rise of Local School Supervision in Massachusetts

Teachers College, Columbia University
Contributions to Education

Vol. I. No. 3.

The Rise of Local School Supervision in Massachusetts

(The School Committee, 1635–1827)

By

Henry Suzzallo, Ph.D.

Assistant Professor of Education, Leland Stanford, Jr., University
Sometime Fellow and Lecturer in Teachers College, Columbia University

Published by Teachers College, Columbia University
New York

January, 1906 **Price, $1.00**

CONTENTS

THE RISE OF

LOCAL SCHOOL SUPERVISION IN MASSACHUSETTS

(THE SCHOOL COMMITTEE, 1635-1827)

CHAPTER I

INTRODUCTION

THE development of school supervision in the commonwealth of Massachusetts accompanied the evolution of a state system of public schools. As more and more public money was devoted to the fostering of education, it was natural that the people should desire to control and supervise the schools to which such money was given. The outcome of the increasing support of education was a system of public schools. The outcome of the tendency in the direction towards controlling the schools supported by public funds was the evolution of the special functions and agencies of school supervision.

At first the supervision of schools was a very simple matter; it had to do largely with matters of support, hiring a teacher, or providing a place for the school. But the conception of the teaching process carried on within the school by the instructor gradually came to be more complicated. More studies were introduced, newer methods came into practice. The standards for efficient teaching became higher. In consequence more supervision of the teaching activity seemed necessary. This complication of the educational idea simply added force to the movement for special agencies and functions of supervision.

At first, when neither the business nor the teaching aspect of a school was regarded as a difficult matter, the people, as a whole, in their town meeting, attended to it well enough. As the notion of the whole business of education came to demand special and frequent attention, the power was delegated to the selectmen, who were the town's representatives, or to the ministers, who were the town's learned men having a special interest in education. But even these individuals with other distracting duties could not satisfy the demands, and special school officials came to be created.

The special school officials which came into existence were the school committeemen and the school superintendents. The development of each has marked a significant period in the growth of local supervision. The school committee came first, and was, in a sense, evolved from the town meeting, as the superintendent was later evolved from the school committee. The rise of the school committee marked the earlier period, from the first educational foundations of the Massachusetts colonies to about the year 1827. The rise of the school superintendent marked the later period, from about the year 1827 to the present time. To trace the rise of these two agencies of school supervision is the twofold purpose of this study.

Each of these sets of school officials presents in its evolution the same characteristic stages of development, four in number. They are as follows: (1) The general body, out of which the agency evolved, began to delegate its power to a person or group of persons, usually members of its own body, for a limited period of time and without the creation of a specific office; (2) individual towns or cities created an official position, incorporating the powers previously delegated, on their own initiative, without the express sanction of the general law of the commonwealth; (3) the state passed a law, permissive in its nature, which sanctioned, tacitly at least, the creation of such offices by the cities or towns; and (4) the state finally required all towns, districts, or cities to establish and maintain the office.

To trace the development of the school committee through these four characteristic stages during the earlier period, is the first purpose of this study. The rise of the school committee in

Massachusetts, while no less significant than the rise of the school superintendent at a later time, is of far greater interest, because so little is known regarding the whole movement. The period of its development is the transitional period of American education and of American political life. It reaches back into the beginnings of American education, and exhibits centuries of groping after educational and political means of controlling the school and its affairs.

To trace the rise of the school committee means to trace, to some extent at least, the control of the town meeting over the public schools, the delegation of educational authority to the selectmen, and the participation of the ministers and others in matters that concerned the school, for all these agencies were closely related to the development of special and term school committees in that period of educational history when the public school system was in the earliest stages of its making. In fact, these agencies were the preliminary means, tried for a time and found wanting, as the school committee was a more nearly final means, which was tried and not found wanting. The agencies taken together in the order of their periods of predominance in school affairs mark the movement wherein school authority is delegated from the more directly representative body to the less directly representative agents of the whole town, from the town's established agencies of political control to new means, called into existence by new needs.

To trace this movement of power from the town meeting, through selectmen, ministers, special committees, and others, to the annually elected committees, is to trace the movement toward more effective school supervision through its first important stage of development. To be sure, such supervision as was exercised by all these various authorities, and even by the early annual committees, is not such supervision of schools as is found in the schools of to-day. But such as it was, it was the basis of the more modern movement. The elements of modern school supervision were involved in some crude manner in even the first votes of the town meetings.

In those days, the school business was simple. It consisted of a vote of support for a teacher, and an additional vote selecting the teacher who was to perform the work. Yet even those two votes represent an early differentiation in school management. In that early vote of support are implied those powers and duties of school administration which have always remained for the large part, in the hands of the layman-officials in school affairs. In the other early vote of electing the teacher are implied those powers and duties of school supervision which have passed, or are, by slow degrees, passing into the hands of a professional class of educational workers.

The development of supervisory powers has been the result largely of the multiplication of functions concerning the teacher and his work. The development of special agencies for school management was largely the result of the same thing. The first powers which were delegated to special authorities were the certification of the teacher, the inspection of the teacher's work, the hiring of the teacher. Matters of school administration, of the business management of the school, as involved in that early vote of school support, were delegated very slowly. At least the first development of the school committee is not predominantly correlated with it.

But it must not be supposed that either the history of the function of school supervision, or the history of the agency of the school committee, can be studied merely from a point of view which is largely modern. While the distinction between school supervision and school administration is perfectly clear to-day, and an early tendency towards differentiation may be noticed, the early colonists were probably not cognizant of such a distinction. Hence, there is in the earliest periods of school control a close, and, very frequently, undifferentiated association of administrative and supervisory activities. In consequence, any study of the rise of the school committee, as the main agency for the exercise of supervisory powers, must involve considerable treatment of the administrative matters which were so closely connected with it.

As a study of supervision involves some consideration of administration, a study of local supervision in the towns and cities of Massachusetts will necessitate more than a treatment of merely local activities. In the history of the subject it is found that the commonwealth through its General Court has expressed an attitude, which has become increasingly definite, with relation to the local management of schools. While educational supervision has been the product of many forces, their influence has been felt largely through two channels. On the one hand, the individual communities have, by their own initiative, tended to create such powers and agencies of supervision in response to local need. On the other hand, the central government has exerted its influence from above, to meet certain needs of the commonwealth as a whole. Through about two centuries, the local governments and the General Court were at work upon the agencies of local school supervision. The final product, the school committee, was the product of both forces. Its evolution can be rightly understood only as both sources of legislation are studied.

CHAPTER II

THE CONTROL OF THE TOWN MEETING

There were two agencies through which the Massachusetts colonists of the early seventeenth century could exert a legislative influence upon the education of that time. There was the General Court for matters of legislation expressing the will of the colony of Massachusetts Bay, and the town meetings of the various towns. They were both agencies of general political control, through which civil, ecclesiastical, educational, and other matters of common interest were treated.

There were certain laws having an educational bearing, passed almost at the very beginning of the commonwealth.[1] But the General Court passed no general law requiring schools until the year 1647.[2] In consequence the earliest recorded attempts at school control are to be found in the town records prior to the year 1647.

It might be expected that the various towns, left to act out of their own initiative, might present a varying practice, and this they did. The variation existed, not only as to the extent of the school control exercised, but likewise as to the particular method by which the town came to establish and regulate its schools. Thus Boston, in 1635, practically established its school by entreating "our brother Philemon Pormont . . . to become scholemaster, for the teaching and nourtering of children."[3]

[1] *Records of Mass.*, ii., 6, 7, 99, 167. [2] *Ibid.*, ii., 203.
[3] Boston, *Rep. Rec. Com.*, ii., 5.

Dedham, in 1642, projected its school, not by electing a teacher in its initial action, but by providing the necessary support for a schoolmaster through an act which set aside school land.[1] Cambridge, in 1638, laid its educational foundation by doing both. Its first vote gave certain lands to the school, for "the vse of mr Nath Eaten as long as he shall be Imployed" in the work of teaching school.[2]

The variation was as extensive in the means used in regulating the school as it was in bringing it into existence. For many decades Watertown, though it had selectmen,[3] controlled its school affairs, with the single exception of ordering a letter written in the year 1649,[4] directly and exclusively through the town meeting.[5] Dorchester in its first school record, in 1639, distributed certain powers not only to its selectmen, but to the elders as well.[6]

The extent of regulation of the internal affairs of the school showed the same tendency towards divergency. Some towns did little more than to vote upon the teacher, his support, and the management of the school lands which were the basis, in large part, of such support. Of these Boston is a good example. From 1635 on, till the end of the century, the internal affairs of the school seem not to have been a matter of general concern.[7] Dorchester, on the other hand, tended to do the opposite from the very beginning. As early as 1645, "the maior p'te of the Inhabitants" adopted certain detailed "rules and orders" concerning the school which applied not only to the teacher, his support and election, the fuel to keep the schoolhouse warm, but also to the hours of instruction, the time for religious catechizing, the use of corporal punishment, etc.[8]

These variations in the method of conducting school affairs were more than merely the record of adjustments which were peculiar to certain places. In some cases, they were the product of differing notions as to the proper method of school

[1] Dedham, *Records*, i., 92.
[2] Cambridge, *Records*, p. 33.
[3] Watertown, *Records*, pp. 1, 2, 6, 8, 10.
[4] *Ibid.*, p. 18.
[5] *Ibid.*, pp. 21, 22, 26, 31, 34–36, 40 *et seq.*
[6] Boston, *Rep. Rec. Com.*, iv., 39.
[7] *Ibid.*, ii., 5 *et seq.*; vii., 22.
[8] *Ibid.*, iv., 54–57.

control, and marked the beginnings of movements which in a later period assumed a widespread significance. In many cases, to be sure, there were variations due to the mere factor of individual initiative alone. Not representing any vital principle in school organization and management, they gave way to others that did, making the way more easy for a tendency toward uniformity, which existed from the beginning, and became most powerful in the period of Massachusetts statehood.

In spite of all the variations noted, there was from the earliest colonial days some tendency toward uniformity of action in school affairs. Socially the Massachusetts colonists were a homogeneous people. They were English, and, more than that, they were English religious dissenters, dominated most intensely by common religious convictions, in a time when religious convictions were unusually strong bonds. The demand for education among them came out of this very religion which bound them together. Education was a religious necessity. To the extent that a common nationality and a common religion existed among them, there was some tendency toward a general interpretation of educational needs which many of the colonists held together. When they came to the means of educational control and supervision, they had the traditions of long-established English practice to start with.[1]

The tendency toward a certain uniformity is clearly discernible even before the unifying influence of the legislation of the General Court was exerted. The most significant fact that appeared in the period prior to the law of 1647 is that, in general, educational control was centred in the inhabitants of a given community as a whole. The political machinery for the expression of their joint will was the town meeting. At this time the people managed their own school affairs, dominantly by direct vote. The Law of 1647, in placing the responsibility for schools upon the town as a whole, recognized the practice most current among the towns.

Specifically, the town meeting, rather than any delegated authority of the inhabitants of the community, tended, in the earliest years of colonial life, to choose the schoolmaster and to provide for his support,—the two most fundamental acts in

[1] *Cf.* Eggleston, *Transit of Civilization*, chap. v., "The Tradition of Education."

the establishment and maintenance of a school as it was then conceived.

Charlestown was one of the earliest to vote school support in its town meeting. In 1636, Lovell's Island, which had been granted by the General Court, was set aside for the school.[1] Cambridge in 1638, entered a memorandum concerning land to be devoted to the school, and assigned it to the use of the schoolmaster.[2] Dorchester, in an extensive order of its town meeting, did a similar thing. In 1639 it imposed forever an annual rental of thirty pounds upon the inhabitants of "Tomsons Iland" "to bee payd to such a schoolemaster as shall undertake to teach."[3] In the same year Newbury granted to Anthony Somerby "foure akers of upland," and "sixe akers of salt marsh," as an "encouragement to keepe schoole for one yeare."[4] Boston, in 1641, followed the precedent of both Charlestown and Dorchester and contributed Deare Island to the support of the Boston Latin School.[5] Finally, the town of Dedham, in the year 1644, decided "yt the remainder of ye Training ground be improued . . . for ye vse of the Fre Schole in the sd towne."[6]

While the general tendency of the town as a whole directly to care for the support seems to be established, there were exceptions among important communities. While a Boston town-meeting gave Deare Island to the support of the town school in 1641, an earlier record of support granted by subscription in 1636 shows that it was done, not at a town meeting of all the freemen, but at a "general meeting of the richer inhabitants."[7] Even in this case the vote was that of a "general meeting" of interested persons. The old town of Roxbury presented another departure from the usual practice. A famous old covenant regarding "the Free Schoole in Roxburie" was agreed upon by a number of "donors (Inhabitantes of the said Towne)."[8] In this case, as in that of Boston in 1636, the covenant was probably the work of the richer inhabitants of the community, rather

[1] Barnard, *Amer. Jour. of Educ.*, xxvii., 127.

[2] Cambridge, *Records*, p. 33.

[3] Boston, *Rep. Rec. Com.*, iv., 39.

[4] Coffin, *History of Newbury*, p. 32.

[5] Boston, *Rep. Rec. Com.*, ii., 92.

[6] Dedham, *Records*, i., 108.

[7] Boston, *Rep. Rec. Com.*, ii., 160, footnote.

[8] Dilliway, *Free schoole of 1645 in Roxburie*, pp. 6–9

than of all the freemen. In the case of Boston, the practice seems to have been limited to the specific case mentioned, the town-meeting assuming the function in other instances. In the case of Roxbury, the control passed into the hands of feoffees, provided for in the covenant, the whole procedure partaking of the nature of a corporation engaged in the establishment of a school, rather than of a town establishing a public town institution.

Not only did the town as a whole contribute support to the school, which in many cases meant direct contribution to the schoolmaster, but the town meeting elected the teacher in most places in the thirties and early forties of the seventeenth century. Numerous instances are upon record. The town of Boston selected Philemon Pormont in 1635.[1] A year later Charlestown arranged with William Witherell "to keep a school for a twelvemonth" and fixed his salary at forty pounds a year.[2] Two years later than Charlestown, Cambridge established, or at least ratified, such establishment of its schoolmaster, "mr Nath Eaten," by giving him the use of ecrtain school lands "as long as he shall be Imployed in that work."[3] The same practice is found among other towns. In 1639, Newbury named its schoolmaster, Anthony Somerby, in making a grant of land to him for his services as schoolmaster for one year.[4] Dorchester, in the same year, while it did not elect a teacher, distinctly ordered that "the sayd schoolmaste [is] to bee chosen fro tyme to tyme p the freemen."[5] In 1640, there was the record that at "a generall towne meeting," held in Salem, "yong Mr. Norris [was] chose by this assembly to teach schoole."[6]

There are certain exceptions to be noted in the matter of the election of teacher, as in the provision of school support. That single record of a "general meeting of the richer inhabitants" of Boston, previously referred to, not only made subscription "towards the maintenance of a free school master," but Mr. Daniel Maud was "also chosen thereunto."[7] In the case of

[1] Boston, *Rep. Rec. Com.*, ii., 5.
[2] Barnard, *Amer. Jour. of Educ.*, xxvii., 127.
[3] Cambridge, *Records*, p. 33.
[4] Coffin, *History of Newbury*, p. 32.
[5] Boston, *Rep. Rec. Com.*, iv., 39.
[6] Felt, *Annals of Salem*, i., 427.
[7] Boston, *Rep. Rec. Com.*, ii., 160, footnote.

Roxbury, the famous covenant of 1645 definitely provided that the persons selected as feoffees "shall have power to putt in or remove the Schoolemaster."[1] Dorchester, which in 1639 had distinctly ordered that the freemen should elect the teacher, in 1645 made it the business of certain wardens or overseers to see that the "sayd Schoole may frō tyme to tyme bee supplied with an able and sufficient Schoolemaster." But the town further ordered that the person provided "is not to be admitted into the place of Schoolemaster without the Generall cōsent of the Inhabitants or the maior p'te of them."[2] This leaves the final control of the election of the schoolmaster where it was before. The function of the wardens was merely to nominate.

It is not an accidental thing that the towns should early show a certain uniform method of providing support for the teacher and electing one. These were the two fundamental acts in the establishment of the school of that time. The school of the early seventeenth century was a simple thing. It consisted largely of some one to teach and some to be taught. Complex systems of education, with costly plants, complicated courses of study, elaborate methods for licensing teachers, skilled bodies of administrators and supervisors, there were none. The choice of one "able to instruct youth" and the payment of his service were the two essential duties of the community. Hence, in general, the freemen of the town attended to both of these matters at their common gathering. In time, as school affairs tended to become more complex, there was a growing tendency to delegate some of the special duties which grew out of these two types of town vote. The tendency existed only in a slight degree in the period prior to 1647. Consequently, when the General Court of the colony came to pass its first general law in 1647, requiring the establishment of schools, it did not delegate the responsibility to any existing body of officials: it charged the "town" or "township" as a whole with the responsibility. The portion of the law which is of concern here is as follows:

It is therefore ordred, yt evry township in this iurisdiction, aftr ye Lord hath increased ym to ye number of fifty householdrs, shall then forthwth appoint one wthin their towne to teach all such children as shall resort to him to write & reade, whose wages shall be paid eithr by

---

[1] Dillaway, *Free Schoole of 1645 in Roxburie*, p. 8.

[2] Boston, *Rep. Rec. Com.*, iv., 54.

ye parents or mastrs of such children, or by ye inhabitants in genrall, by way of supply, as ye maior pt of those yt ordr ye prudentials of ye towne shall appoint; provided, those yt send their children be not oppressed by paying much more yn they can have ym taught for in othr townes; and it is furthr ordered, yt where any towne shall increase to ye numbr of one hundred families or househouldrs they shall set up a gramer schoole, ye master thereof being able to instruct youth so farr as they may be fited for ye university; provided, yt if any towne neglect ye performance hereof above one yeare, yt every such towne shall pay 5£ to ye next schoole till they shall performe this order.[1]

It will be noticed that in both the founding of schools and the election of teachers, the legal obligation is placed upon the town as a whole, not upon any special officer or set of officers. It is the "towne" that "shall set up a gramer schoole." It is the "township" which "shall then forthwth appoint one wthin their towne to teach." It is the "towne shall pay 5£" in case "any towne neglect ye performance hereof above one yeare." And such levying of responsibility by the General Court in its first compulsory school law was the recognition of the general local practice.

The law contains certain other statements and implications which may be noted, as they have to do with the detailed factors involved in the two above-named acts of the town. (1) The particular method by which such support was to be raised was. left optional. The teacher's "wages shall be paid eithr by ye parents or mastrs of such children, or by ye inhabitants in genrall, by way of supply." (2) The law implied that the teachers appointed by the town should have certain qualifications. Certain abilities were recognized in the grading of the schools into two groups, and in the mention of their function in terms of varying definiteness. The law says that the elementary school teacher is "to teach all such children as shall resort to him to write & reade." In the case of the grammar or secondary school teacher it states, "ye master thereof being able to instruct youth so farr as they may be fited for ye university."

Just what relation these two further implications of the law bear to the local practice of the various towns prior to 1647 is difficult to state. The use of the profits of the town school lands, as previously stated, was common. But there is no record sufficiently illuminating upon either the contribution of

[1] *Records of Mass.*, ii., 203.

parents and masters of children to the school expense, or upon the detailed manner of selecting a teacher at this time in the town records of Boston, Cambridge, Dorchester, or Dedham; all of which towns legislated upon school affairs prior to the date of this law. In the twofold responsibility of the town for the provision of some means that a school might be set up and for the appointment of a teacher, many of the complex actions of modern education are in a way involved. As the social demands upon the school become greater through the centuries, and the work of the school responds through a more subtle and complex machinery, the specialized agencies of educational control and supervision come into existence. The historic beginnings of it all are in these simple votes of the colonial towns. The Massachusetts town of to-day still votes its support in the town meeting much as it did in the early seventeenth century.[1] But it is far different with the powers that were then merged in the simple election or re-election of the teacher by the town-meeting. The latter action, the supplying of the school "with an able and sufficient Schoolemaster,"[2] buried within itself the functions of certification, appointment, assignment, and, where a teacher was reappointed to his place, inspection and supervision. The appointment of a teacher involved, unconsciously to be sure, the first three factors in modern school supervision. His reappointment also involved the two more purely educational factors; however such inspection was founded upon the chance visits of some freeman bent upon seeing his truant son to school, or upon the idle babblings of the children to their parents at the close of school. And the town supervised its school by the annual or term vote which expressed a supervisory opinion formulated upon just such chance and unreliable data.

In time the state demanded a more or less sharp differentiation of the powers that have been suggested as lying buried in the vote which appointed the teacher. It came later to treat the whole question of the support of the school with more careful detail. But that action of the state was late in coming. As education became more complex, the various powers or functions began to differentiate and were gradually delegated to

[1] *Revised Laws of Mass.*, 1904, chap. xlii, sec. 22, p. 19.

[2] Boston, *Rep. Rec. Com.*, iv., 54.

particular officers rather than to the town as a whole. Not until 1693 did the General Court lay the responsibility "for the settlement and maintenance of such schoolmaster and masters" anywhere else than upon the inhabitants of the town in general. In that year it divided the responsibility, or, at least, laid it in two places,—upon "the selectmen and the inhabitants of such towns." The law reads as follows:

> That every town within this province, having the number of fifty householders or upwards, shall be constantly provided of a schoolmaster to teach children and youth to read and write. And where any town or towns have the number of one hundred families or householders, there shall also be a grammar school set up in every such town, and some discreet person of good conversation, well instructed in the tongues, procured to keep such school. Every such schoolmaster to be suitably encouraged and paid by the inhabitants. And the selectmen and the inhabitants of such towns, respectively, shall take effectual care and make due provision for the settlement and maintenance of such schoolmaster and masters.[1]

As late as 1671 a law was passed which placed the responsibility for the setting up of schools and the appointment of masters upon the town as a whole, exactly as the act of 1647 had done. No mention is made of selectmen in this law, a portion of which reads: "Whereas the law requires euery towne, consisting of one hundred familjes or vpward, to sett vp a grammar schoole, & appointe a master thereof; . . ."[2]

A still later law of the General Court, that of 1683, made the same assumption. It reads:

> As an addition to the law, title Schooles, this Court doth order and enact, that euery towne consisting of more than fiue hundred familjes or householders shall set vp & mainteyne two gram̄er schooles and two wrighting schooles, the masters whereof shall be fitt and able to instruct youth as sajd law directs; . . ."[3]

In Plymouth, which was separate from Massachusetts Bay, until the year 1691,[4] the tendency was the same as in its sister colony. The law of 1658, which urged the support of schools, made its appeal to the "Towne" or "Townshipes."

[1] Mass., *Prov. Acts & Res.*, i., 63.
[2] *Records of Mass.*, iv., pt. 2, p. 486.
[3] *Ibid.*, v., 414, 415.
[4] Winsor, *Narrative and Critical History of America*, iii., 282.

> It is proposed by the Court vnto the seuerall Townshipes of this Jurisdiction as a thinge they ought to take into serious consideration that some course may be taken that in euery Towne there may be a Scoolmaster sett vp to traine vp children to reading and writing.[1]

Later, when the General Court of Plymouth made the provision of schools compulsory, the responsibility was laid upon the town as in the much earlier laws of Massachusetts Bay. This law of 1677 begins, "This Court doth therefor order; that in whatsoeuer Townshipp in this Gou'ment consisting of fifty families or vpwards; any meet man shal be obtained to teach a Gramer scoole. . . ."[2]

The tendency of the town-meeting to give up some of the management of school affairs by placing it upon the selectmen, which, as will be seen later, was gradually developing among the towns, through their own initiative, received some recognition from the General Court before the law of 1693. In 1654 it commended it to the care of "the selectmen in the seuerall townes, not to admitt or suffer any such to be contynued in the office or the place of teaching, educating or instructing of youth or child, in the colledge or schooles, that haue manifested y^m^selves vnsound in the fayth, or scandelous in theire liues, & not giueing due satisfaction according to the rules of Christ."[3] While there was nothing obligatory in the act, it was nevertheless a sanction to the assumption of some authority on the part of selectmen with reference to the qualifications of schoolmasters that might be hired by the town.

While the General Court was recognizing more and more the authority of the selectmen in school affairs, the towns were definitely delegating more and more power to them. This was quite marked in the period from about 1647 to the year 1692/3, when the law was passed which made the town and the selectmen jointly responsible for the "settlement and maintenance" of schoolmasters.[4]

The town records of Boston from 1644 to 1689 are practically the record of what the selectmen did in school affairs, or of what the town instructed or permitted them to do.[5] There are

[1] *Plymouth Col. Rec.*, xi., 142.

[2] *Ibid.*, xi., 246, 247.

[3] *Records of Mass.*, iii., 343, 344.

[4] Mass., *Prov. Acts & Res.*, i., 63.

[5] Boston, *Rep. Rec. Com.*, ii., 86, 92, 94, 95, 97, 99, 125, 126, 129, 130, 133, 140, 142; vii., 22, 24, 30, 32, 33, 36, 38, 51, 53, 57, 63, 127, 158, 161, 171, 183, 184, 191, 192.

some exceptions, however, but they are scattered. In 1650 the town fixed the salary of "Mr Woodmansey, the Schoolmaster."[1] In 1669/70 the town granted his widow seven pounds, provided she vacated the schoolhouse.[2] In 1689 the old-time authority of the town meeting in school affairs seems to have been returned, temporarily, at least, by the following motion: "Voted that the former Custome & practice in managing the affairs of the free schools be restored & continued." [3]

The town of Cambridge, from 1662 to 1691, recorded no action in educational matters at its town meeting. Such action as is recorded is given as part of the proceedings of the selectmen.[4]

The town of Dorchester elected a schoolmaster at a town meeting in 1665.[5] After that time, until 1683, when the printed record ceases, there is no record of the election of a teacher by the town. The power "to looke out after," "agree with," or "hire a schoolmaster" is delegated to some set of officials or to some committee.[6] The town meeting released the schoolmaster in 1669, in order that he might become a minister to the people at Hadley.[7] There was evidently some action of the town bearing on the support of the school,[8] though even here the evidence is not clear as to the general practice. The selectmen may have levied the rate.[9]

Dedham is another example of a town where the town meeting tended gradually, in this period, to relieve itself of certain functions which had to do with the operation of the school, particularly with those involved in the selection and hiring of a teacher. In 1658 the town hired a teacher and asked that the selectmen "agree" with him.[10] After that time and until the close of the printed record in 1673, the votes of the town on educational matters are limited.[11] In 1660 the town voted "that

[1] Boston, *Rep. Rec. Com.*, ii., 99. [2] *Ibid.*, vii., 53. [3] *Ibid.*, vii., 197.

[4] Cambridge, *Records*, pp. 138, 180, 182, 188, 293, 296.

[5] Boston, *Rep. Rec. Com.*, iv., 128.

[6] *Ibid.*, iv., 136, 143, 145, 146, 151, 155, 159, 188, 198, 200, 208–210, 221, 223, 236, 245, 251, 255–257, 267, 268.

[7] *Ibid.*, iv., 159.

[8] *Ibid.*, iv., 146, 221.

[9] *Ibid.*, iv., 267.

[10] Dedham, *Records*, ii., 2.

[11] *Ibid.*, ii., 2–4, 6, 16, 26, 27, 29, 32, 35, 42, 46, 48, 67, 68, 72, 83, 91 112, 116, 120, 125, 133 140, 146, 155, 156, 160, 162, 171, 180, 194 199, 205, 221, 222, 224, 225.

the publike schoole . . . shall be continued."[1] In 1661 it records a similar vote of the freemen, and "further it is voated that the select men . . . shall prouide a schoolemaster if thay can atayne one."[2] It would seem that much of the school control was handled outside the town meeting; the town exercised some supervision by passing on the acts of its officers, as in the case of the selectmen whose acts were passed upon by the town in 1666.[3]

While it was true that the town meetings exercised direct control over school affairs to a lessened extent, allowing the selectmen to care for the details of school management, a fact which the general law of 1692/3 recognized, there were certain exceptions to the general tendency, as might be expected. A very notable exception was Watertown. The first records of the town, in 1649, show a committee of one on the building of a school house, and that the selectmen were probably delegated to get a schoolmaster.[4] In 1650 the town elected a schoolmaster and agreed with him.[5] After that time until 1673, an almost unbroken record shows that the town, and not any delegated authority, "agreed" with the schoolmaster annually.[6]

It is to be noted, then, that the towns in the seventeenth century tended less and less to attend to the details of school affairs through the town meeting. In general, the town delegated many school matters to some other authority. The General Court in turn recognized the existing tendency in the formulation of its laws concerning the establishment and maintenance of schools by towns.

This tendency, which has been traced up to the year 1693, naturally continued through the succeeding provincial period, until finally, in the early period of statehood, a distinct political organization for the conduct of school affairs was brought into existence under the sanction of the central government. It has been suggested that, of the two characteristic votes of the earli-

[1] Dedham, *Records*, ii., 29.

[2] *Ibid*., ii., 42.

[3] *Ibid*., ii., 125.

[4] Watertown, *Records*, p. 18.

[5] *Ibid*., pp. 21, 22.

[6] *Ibid*., pp. 26, 31, 35, 36, 40, 43, 55, 60, 64, 70, 74, 79, 84, 91, 93, 96, 102, 109, 113, 117.

est town meetings, the Massachusetts town of to-day has practically retained in the old form the right and the duty of voting support for schools through the town meeting. Those other powers, which were in a sense implied in that other characteristic vote of choosing the teacher, the powers of certification, appointment, assignment, inspection, and supervision in general, were those which, as they tended to emerge as distinct types of functions, the town gradually gave up to some delegated authority. They finally came into the hands of the school committees.

Since the tracing of the movement toward delegation of authority and the movement toward the establishment of the school committees are to be treated elsewhere, it suffices at this point merely to sketch the lessening control of the town meeting in this later period. Since all the powers for the operation of town schools by the local authority were by implication vested in the town meeting in the beginning, and since there was this gradual tendency of the individual towns to give over certain of their powers and duties, which the educational statutes of the commonwealth recognized, the control of the town in the third period (1693–1827) may be best indicated for our present purposes by a somewhat negative treatment. It may be shown, by tracing, through the statutes of the General Court, the sequence with which other bodies than the town meeting came to exercise special educational powers formerly performed in the general assembly of the town.

In the previous period, the General Court had made some recognition of the tendency of the town to delegate its authority and duty. In 1654 it did "commend it" to the selectmen to see that teachers possessed a moral and religious character.[1] In 1692/3 one law held "the selectmen and the inhabitants" of towns responsible for the "settlement and maintenance" of teachers.[2] Another law of the same year gave selectmen power to assess for schools on vote of "major part" of inhabitants,[3] legalizing a prevailing custom.[4] But no one of these acts had delegated any particular power or duty to any particular person or persons to be performed by them by authority of their office

[1] *Records of Massachusetts*, iii., 343, 344.

[2] Mass., *Prov. Acts & Res.*, i., 63.

[3] *Ibid.*, i., 66.

[4] Boston, *Rep. Rec. Com.*, iv., 55.

and as an obligation to the community. Such a tendency is not definitely noted until after 1693.

The law of June 25, 1701/2, on the certification of the "grammar-school master," is the first legal recognition of one of the special powers which evolved from the early town vote of electing the teacher. It is the first definite placing of a particular educational power in the hands of a special set of officials. It is the first certain and definite subtraction of power from the town as a whole. It placed the power of certification in the hands of a majority of the ministers of the town and its two adjacent towns.[1]

The precedent laid down by the law of 1701/2 was followed in 1711/2 by another act which applied the same principle to the certification of elementary teachers.[2] In this case the delegation of authority was, not to the ministers, but to the selectmen of the town in which the school was to be kept. Thus the entire power of determining the minimum standard for judging the fitness of a person to become a schoolmaster of the town was taken from the hands of the town as a whole and placed in the hands of special officials.

The town had been the only recognized unit for the support of schools from the beginning. In 1767/8 the precincts, districts, or ecclesiastical subdivisions of the town were allowed to tax themselves for schools, schoolmasters, and schoolhouses through the annual meeting of the inhabitants of the precinct.[3] Thus the town meeting was compelled to share one of its original privileges, and there was established another unit for school management. In 1789 the general law requiring schools laid the responsibility for the provision of schoolmasters upon "every town or district,"[4] thus reiterating the effect of the previous law. In time the town became again the sole basis for the local support of schools, but not until after a hard struggle lasting through many decades.[5]

The law of 1789 not only sanctioned either the "town or district" as the unit for local school maintenance, but, in a

[1] Mass., *Prov. Acts & Res.*, i., 470.

[2] *Ibid.*, i., 681, 682.

[3] *Ibid.*, iv., 988.

[4] Mass., *Perpetual Laws*, ii., 39, 40.

[5] Martin, *Evolution of the Mass. Public School System*, p. 205.

somewhat amended form, it sanctioned the previous delegation of the power of certification to the ministers and selectmen.[1] It did more than this, it sanctioned certain customs which had been growing up among the towns, without definitely placing the power in any particular place. Finally, it definitely delegated certain powers to particular authorities other than the town as a whole.

There had been a strong tendency among the towns toward the appointment of special school committees. They were appointed for various purposes connected with the school, sometimes merely to attend to some matter which required transient attention; sometimes for a regular term to give continued attention to school matters. Of the committees of the first type a few may be mentioned. In 1747 Duxbury appointed a committee of one as "their Agent to procure a School master." [2] In 1750 Lunenberg appointed a committee of five to locate the sites of schoolhouses.[3] Dudley, in 1760, appointed a committee of three to sell the schoolhouse.[4] In 1762, Brookline appointed a committee of five to care for a legacy left to the school.[5] In the same year Braintree appointed a committee of three "to examine into the state of the School." [6]

Of the second type of school committees, those that were elected at regular intervals and evidently holding office for a specified term, the following cases may be noted: Boston had a committee on visitation of schools from 1721 on.[7] Fitchburg annually appointed a committee of five or six from 1774 till the time of the law of 1789.[8] Dudley had a committee of seven, evidently appointed each year from 1772 till the enactment of the law mentioned.[9] The law of 1789 recognized these committees in the treatment of the subject of certification by accepting the certificate of the "committee of such parish or place"

[1] Mass., *Perpetual Laws*, ii., 41–43.

[2] Duxbury, *Records*, p. 277.

[3] Lunenberg, *Records*, p. 141.

[4] Dudley, *Records*, ii., 49.

[5] Brookline, *Records*, i., 204.

[6] Braintree, *Records*, p. 383.

[7] Boston, *Rep. Rec. Com.*, xii., 14 *et seq.;* xiv., 9 *et seq.;* xvi., 10, *et seq.;* xviii., 24 *et seq.*

[8] Fitchburg, *Records*, i., 101 *et seq.;* ii., 20 *et seq.*

[9] Dudley, *Records*, p. 137 *et seq.*

in lieu of one from the selectmen.[1] These committees are mentioned in connection with the function of visitation in the same optional relationship with the selectmen.[2] Nowhere, however, does the law specifically state that towns or districts may have such committees.

Many of these committees mentioned above, both the temporary and term committees, had as their function the procuring or hiring of schoolmasters. This was the case with Duxbury and others, which appointed temporary committees; and also with Dudley, Fitchburg, and others appointing annual committees. In other towns the selectmen usually hired the schoolmaster. The town meeting of Boston in 1784 authorized its selectmen to appoint a schoolmaster, "if they shall judge it" to necessary to have one.[3] In 1787, it was voted by the inhabitants of Brookline that the selectmen "Ingage a School mistress to keep School."[4]

This power of the towns to delegate the choosing and hiring of teachers to selectmen and committees was also given a sanction by this law. The sanction is entirely by implication in this case, as well as in the authorization of special school committees. Such power is referred to in the section on certification of grammar and other school masters where the following clause occurs, "such Selectmen or Committee, who may be authorized to hire such schoolmaster."[5]

But the framers of this law went farther than to restate the provisions of previous laws and to sanction the practices which had become widespread among the towns. New powers in educational supervision were given specific recognition and delegated to specific officers of the town by state law. Section three of this important law practically gave the selectmen the power to determine the grade of schools in certain cases. The law directed that children shall not be admitted to grammar schools unless they are able "to read the English language, by spelling the same," thus practically setting off the grammar school from the elementary school. But the selectmen were given the option of making a given school both secondary and elementary in one, for the law reads further: "or the Selectmen of the town where

[1] Mass., *Perpetual Laws*, ii., 41.
[2] *Ibid.*, ii., 42, 43.
[3] Boston, *Rep. Rec. Com.*, xxxi., 60.
[4] Brookline, *Records*, i., 357.
[5] Mass., *Perpetual Laws*, ii., 41.

such grammar school is, shall direct the grammar school master to receive and instruct such youth," [1] that is, children of elementary grade.

The other power which this law definitely differentiated from school control in general was that of visitation and inspection. The annually appointed committee of Boston mentioned above was a committee on visitation.[2] Springfield, as early as 1735, had appointed a committee "to take the Inspection and Regulation of the School" on the west side of the river.[3] Fitchburg gave its school committee supervisory power over the teachers employed by them in 1776.[4] The law of the General Court made the visitation and inspection of schools a uniform requirement upon the ministers and selectmen or committee "of the several towns and districts." [5]

The constant tendency toward the further differentiation of the powers of school control and of the delegation of them, was emphasized by an act of the year 1800. It did two things of importance. It gave explicitly, for the first time, the power to appoint committees. The particular kind of a committee was designated. The "inhabitants of the several School Districts" were "empowered . . . to choose a Committee to superintend the building and repairing" of schoolhouses.[6] The other provision made it the duty of the selectmen of the town to decide the location of district schoolhouses when the district could not agree. It is important only to the extent that it is another recognition of the whole trend in the management of school affairs at that time.

The first explicit authorization of a school committee to have the general "care and superintendence" of the public schools was in 1822, when the same was authorized for the city of Boston,[7] paving the way for a general law requiring such a school committee for each town.

This law came in 1826, and gave to every town a school committee with "the general charge and superintendence of all the public schools." [8] The rise of the school committee as a

[1] Mass., *Perpetual Laws*, ii., 40.

[2] See above, p. 19.

[3] Springfield, *Records*, ii., 508.

[4] Fitchburg, *Records*, i., 133.

[5] Mass., *Perpetual Laws*, ii., 42, 43.

[6] *Ibid.*, ii., 80.

[7] *Ibid.*, ii., 82.

[8] Mass., *Acts & Resolves*, 1826, chap. clxx., pp. 299–303.

definite body for the care of school affairs left the town meeting with little of its original power. As fast as some special function had been developed, it had been delegated by the towns to some person or persons. The General Court soon sanctioned the practice, or definitely placed it in the hands of some official agency. Now the power to prescribe text-books passed from the town to the school committee,[1] and there was little left to the town meeting beyond the support of schools, except the election of teachers, and this the towns were permitted to delegate to the selectmen or the school committee by the implication of the previous act of 1789.[2]

The law of the following year, that of 1827,[3] which was largely a more detailed formulation of the law of 1826, finally took even the power of appointment of teachers from the town and gave it to the prudential committeeman of the school district.[4]

Thus in less than two centuries the town meeting had given up much of its direct control of the schools. In the earliest days of colonial life, when the school was a very modest affair, the town meeting usually arranged the details of its control. But the school became complicated, and the management of the schools became more than a matter of hiring and supporting a teacher by town vote. Even the matter of support did not remain exclusively to the town, for its districts or subdivisions took this privilege and shared it in common with the town. The powers represented in that vote of the town which elected the teacher became differentiated, and as this occurred they were delegated by the town meeting. Later, the state fixed the responsibility for their performance on some particular town office. First, certification went in the first quarter of the eighteenth century. Then, as the function of visitation and inspection developed, and as the town as a whole could not perform the service, the central legislative authority gave it into the hands of ministers, selectmen, and special committees. Finally, with the first quarter of the nineteenth century, the power of appointing teachers, which had in the beginning involved both certification and supervision, passed from the town

1 Mass., *Acts & Resolves*, 1826, chap. clxx., sec. 2, p. 300.

2 Mass., *Perpetual Laws*, ii., 41.

3 Mass., *Acts & Resolves*, 1827, chap. cxliii., pp. 557–571.

4 *Ibid.*, 1827, chap. cxliii., sec. 6, p. 561.

to the prudential committee. A definite machinery for the exercise of these powers was found in the school committees, and when these were established by compulsory law of the state the town meeting could no longer be considered as the main agency in the management of those matters which concern most directly the teaching function of the school.

CHAPTER III

THE DELEGATION OF POWER TO THE SELECTMEN

In that famous body of laws of the Colony of Massachusetts Bay, known as the *Body of Liberties*, there was not only granted to the "Freemen of every Township . . . power to make such by laws and constitutions as may concern the wellfare of their Towne," in matters of a prudential nature [1]; but this same compilation of the year 1641 contained as one of its "Liberties" a provision for town officers or selectmen, whose business it was to attend to the general affairs of the town under the supervision of the town meeting. This law provides that:

> The freemen of every Towne or Towneship, shall have full power to choose yearly or for lesse time out of themselves a convenient number of fitt men to order the planting or prudentiall occasions of that Town, according to instructions given to them in writeing, Provided nothing be done by them contrary to the publique laws and orders of the Countrie, provided also the number of such select persons be not above nine.[2]

These "select persons" or selectmen, as they were later called, dealt with the same general town matters as the town meeting, exercising themselves with such details as might be committed to them because the town as a whole could not conveniently do so. School affairs were among the prudential affairs of the town, and as the business of the town in general came more and more to be delegated to the selectmen, school matters likewise tended to become the business of the selectmen. The dominant control of the town in the earliest colonial period in matters of school administration has already been noticed. Its gradual delegation of authority has likewise been indicated.

[1] Whitmore, *Colonial Laws*, i., 47; *Liberty* 66.
[2] *Ibid.*, i., 49 ; *Liberty* 74.

Among the various movements towards the vesting of authority in some body outside the town meeting, the one towards placing such power in the hands of the selectmen was the earliest. It is the first step in the evolution of an official authority which will have, as its sole concern, the management of the schools.

When the General Court gave to the communities the right to "make such orders as may concern the well ordering of their own towns," and permitted the towns to select persons to assist in such town business, it provided that such actions should "not be repugnant to the laws and orders . . . established by the General Court."[1] Hence, while matters of local concern were left largely in the hands of the town, when such matters became of importance to the whole commonwealth, the General Court did not hesitate to pass over the town meeting and make its demands directly upon some special official or officials who might really be under the direction of the town meeting, making them in a sense directly responsible to the central government. In many cases this amounted to removing authority from the town as a whole. Such was an order of procedure quite common in the evolution of the school committee.

The first imposition of authority upon the selectmen by the General Court in matters educational was in the law of June 14, 1642, when "This Co^rt, taking into consideration the great neglect of many parents & masters in training up their children in learning, & labr, and other implyments which may be proffitable to the common wealth, do hereupon order and decree, that in euery towne ye chosen men appointed for managing the prudentiall affajres of the same shall henceforth stand charged with the care of the redresse of this evill, . . . to take account from time to time . . . concerning their calling and implyment of their children, especially of their ability to read & understand the principles of religion & the capitall lawes of this country. . . ."[2] In 1668 this law was reiterated.[3]

The above law was by no means a dead letter. There are numerous instances showing that the law was put into effect by the selectmen. They themselves examined the children or deputed some one to do it, and negligent parents were given a hearing by the selectmen. In 1642 Cambridge divided its terri-

[1] Whitmore, *Colonial Laws*, i., 12, 13.

[2] *Records of Mass.*, ii., 6, 7.

[3] *Ibid.*, iv., pt. 2, 395, 396.

tory among the selectmen so that one would be responsible for each portion in carrying out the order of the General Court.[1] In 1670 the selectmen issued an order dividing the town into eight districts, and assigning two persons to each district "for the Cattichising of the youth of the towne." [2] In the same year it is recorded that the selectmen of Watertown gave a hearing to those who had not properly instructed their children.[3] And three years later, in 1673, the selectmen of the same town reported the children who have not been properly taught and catechised.[4] In 1676 the selectmen sent three committees of two each to three different families to see if the "chilldren be taught to Read inglish." [5] In the year 1680 the selectmen of Dorchester appointed "Elder Humphry to Cattechiz the youth and Children." [6]

This practice of looking after the education of youth could not but re-enforce the first-mentioned tendency of the town meeting, to delegate its affairs in general to the selectmen, whenever such seemed necessary. The law with regard to the catechising of children did not give the selectmen any power over schools, to be sure, but it did give some responsibility for public education to the selectmen. From such responsibility for literacy among children, it was a short step to the care of the school which the town might establish, particularly in those detailed functions which the town meeting might be likely to delegate.

Even before the passage of this law, Dorchester, in drawing up regulations for its school in 1639, left it "to the discretion of elders and the 7 men for the tyme beeing whether maydes shalbe taught with the boyes or not." [7] Action on school affairs was more frequent after the law of 1642, though just what influence the law itself had it is difficult to say. The records of the towns which took action in school matters before this date are very meagre. This is true even during the next two or three decades. Boston gives some of the earliest records of the votes of selectmen. In 1644, "at a meeting of men selected to order the affayres of the town, Its ordered that the Constables shall

[1] Cambridge, *Records*, p. 47.
[2] *Ibid.*, p. 188.
[3] Watertown, *Records*, pp. 103, 104.
[4] *Ibid.*, p. 114.
[5] *Ibid.*, p. 128.
[6] Boston, *Rep. Rec. Com.*, iv., 255.
[7] *Ibid.*, iv., 39.

pay unto Deacon Eliot for the use of m^{r} Woodbridge eight pounds due to him for keeping the Schoole the Last yeare."[1] The following year the Constables were ordered to set off part of the rates for the mending of the schoolmaster's fence.[2] In 1647 the same set of officials attended to the rental of Deare Island for seven years,[3] the island having previously been voted to the use of the school.[4] It is impossible to say whether such actions were definitely delegated by the town or not. There is no evidence upon the point, as there is later in the case of this same town. The mere fact is all that can be noted at this time.

The first law of the General Court to give any power to the selectmen in matters that directly touched education in the town schools is the act of November 11, 1647.[5] It is the same act that has been noted as tending to lay the primary responsibility for schools upon towns and townships. But in this law there is a clause which a studied interpretation would show to be a distinct delegation of power to the selectmen. The clause refers to the teacher of reading and writing, "whose wages shall be paid eith^{r} by ye parents or mast^{rs} of such children, or by ye inhabitants in gen^{r} all, by way of supply, as ye maior p^{t} of those y^{t} ord^{r} ye prudentials of ye towne shall appoint."

Since the responsibility in the matter of schools was laid upon the town as a whole in every other part of the law, and the expression in the particular clause cited is somewhat ambiguous, it might be understood that the "maior p^{t} of those y^{t} ord^{r} ye prudentials of ye towne" meant the majority of the freemen privileged to vote in the "prudentiall" affairs of the town.[6] But a study of the terminology used in both the laws of the General Court and the records of the town and selectmen's meetings would seem to confirm the interpretation that the reference was to the selectmen, rather than to the enfranchised inhabitants.

The phrase "those y^{t} ord^{r} ye prudentials of ye towne," practically parallels the phraseology of three previous laws of the central government, in each of which cases the reference to the selectmen is obvious. In the "Body of Liberties," edition of

[1] Boston, *Rep. Rec. Com.*, ii., 82. [2] *Ibid.*, ii., 86.
[3] *Ibid.*, ii., 92. [4] *Ibid.*, ii., 65. [5] *Records of Mass.*, ii., 203.
[6] Whitmore, *Colonial Laws*, i., 47; *Body of Liberties*, 66, also see discussion of the use of the term "prudential," note 7, pp. 12–14.

1641, the section which authorizes the appointments of "select persons" distinctly calls them "fitt men to order the planting or prudentiall occasions of that Town."[1] A law of 1643 refers to the selectmen as "persons . . . that are deputed to order the prudential affajres" of the town.[2] Again, an act of November 4, 1646, denominates the selectmen of the town by the words, "such as are deputed to order the prudentialls thereof."[3]

This interpretation is further borne out by the local records. The Dorchester records for 1634 state that "It is agreed that there shall be Tenn men chosen to order all the affayres of the Plantation."[4] In 1639 the "7 men" are referred to as being for the same purpose. In 1642 and 1644 similar references are made.[5] Boston also made many direct allusions to the selectmen almost in the same terminology as that given above. As early as 1641, the selectmen were named as "chosen to order the Town's occasions."[6] Similar language, where the meaning is perfectly plain, was used in 1644 and 1645 in the records of the same town.[7] The usage of a phrase similar to that in the law in question continued even after the date of this law, though the term "selectmen" had come into somewhat general use.[8] Dedham used the expression in 1647.[9] Watertown, as late as 1673, elected its chosen men and called them "selekt men to ordur the prudenshall afayures of the town," and repeated the reference the following year.[10]

It seems a justifiable assumption that the clause in the act of 1647, which gives to the "maior p^{t} of those y^{t} ord^{r} ye towne" the power to determine how the schoolmaster shall be paid, is the first delegation of power in school affairs made by law of the General Court to the selectmen of the towns. Just how far this power was based upon current practice there is

[1] Whitmore, *Colonial Laws*, i., 47; *Liberty* 66.

[2] *Records of Mass.*, ii., 1–18.

[3] *Ibid.*, ii., 19.

[4] Boston, *Rep. Rec. Com.*, iv., 7.

[5] *Ibid.*, iv., 38, 50, 52.

[6] *Ibid.*, ii., 61.

[7] *Ibid.*, ii., 79, 82, 84.

[8] The term "selectmen" is found in Boston as early as 1643 (*Rep. Rec. Com.*, ii., 76), and in Braintree as early as 1641 (*Records*, p. 2).

[9] Dedham, *Records*, i., 117.

[10] Watertown, *Records*, pp. 117, 121.

practically no evidence to show. Prior to 1647 there seem to have been but two votes of the Boston selectmen which might bear upon the matter. In 1644, and again in 1645, the selectmen ordered certain amounts of money to be set aside by the Constables for the schoolmaster's use in return for his services.[1] Whether these acts of the selectmen, which probably set apart money from the town stock, determined the method of paying the teacher, it is impossible to say. It cannot even be said that these acts were performed either by the initiative of the selectmen or by order of the town. No previous instructions are recorded in the town record, however. The records of Dorchester, Cambridge, and Dedham do not show any similar action by the selectmen.

There is reason for believing that the selectmen did not generally assume the right to say how the schoolmaster should be paid. The earliest instances where the method of payment was determined are votes of the town meeting rather than of the selectmen. In 1650 Boston voted "that M. Woodmansey, the Schoolmaster, shall have fiftye pounds per annum for his teachinge the schollers, and his proportion to be made up by ratte."[2] Cambridge town meeting, in 1648, agreed that the town should pay for the schoolmaster and voted the "sum of ten pounds, if it can be attained" by the sale of land from the Common.[3] In 1654 the same town "consented that twenty pounds should be levied upon the severall Inhabitants and given to mr Corlet."[4] A general town meeting of Dedham, in 1651, resolved that a school should be kept for seven years and agreed "that the settled mayntenance or wages" should be twenty pounds, to be raised as "A Towne stocke," part of which was to be paid by the parents or masters of children of a certain age, and the remainder "Raised by waye of Rateing vpon Estates."[5] Watertown, in 1650, through its town meeting, chose a schoolmaster and agreed "y^t^ the towne did pmise to allowe . . . thirty pounds for this yeare." In 1651 the town meeting designated how much must be paid for the "Inglish" scholars and how much for the "Latten" scholars.[6]

[1] Boston, *Rep. Rec. Com.*, ii., 82, 86.
[2] *Ibid.*, ii., 99.
[3] Cambridge, *Records*, p. 77.
[4] *Ibid.*, p. 106.
[5] Dedham, *Records*, i., 15, 16, 136.
[6] Watertown, *Records*, pp. 21, 26.

All of these instances follow shortly after the passing of the law of 1647. Yet it is evident that if the law intended to put the responsibility upon the selectmen, they certainly did not assume it. In the cases cited, the town certainly did, through its town meeting. Whether this was due to some ambiguity in the law, or to the fact that the law seemed to lay down this requirement merely for the manner of paying the elementary teacher, thus leaving a loophole; or whether it was due to the fact that the town insisted upon attending to matters of important financial concern, it is impossible to state. It might have been any one or all of these facts.

Nor did the selectmen seem to assume this power in a later period than the cases above cited. There are some few instances that show that the selectmen did arrange such matters. But they seem to have been less frequent than cases where the town meeting attended to the matter. In the Dorchester *Records*, in the year 1655, there is a record that might seem to indicate that the selectmen, in agreeing with the teacher, indicated how he was to be paid.[1] But the record is not at all clear. The selectmen might have been merely carrying out the order of the town. In fact, this possibility overshadows most of the instances where the selectmen agree with a teacher and indicate the manner of support. In the case of Dedham, the selectmen were in the habit of agreeing with the teacher, and some mention is made of levying a "Rate to paye the Schoolmaster at 3^{s}–6^{d} each scholler" at a selectmen's meeting in 1664.[2] But it cannot be said that this was a deliberative and not an instructed procedure of the officials of the town. Such an inference would probably seem incorrect in the light of the fact that a town meeting of the year 1666 voted a school rate on "male Childeren that are capeable to paye," and passed on the acts of the selectmen.[3] In 1683 three members of a Boston committee on "Almes and work house" met with the seven selectmen of the town of Boston and agreed that the town should establish two schools, the town to allow twenty-five pounds, and "such psons as send theire Children to schoole (y^{t} are able) should pay somethinge to ye Master for his better incouragement in his

[1] Boston, *Rep. Rec. Com.*, iv., 73, 74.
[2] Dedham, *Records*, ii., 32, 83, 91, 116, 120.
[3] *Ibid.*, ii., 125.

worke."[1] But even this cannot be ascribed to the law in question, for there seemed to be in Boston during this period an unusual local tendency to let the selectmen attend to all school affairs. In fact, from 1655 to 1689, the town registered no vote on school affairs save to refer some school matters to the selectmen.[2] Later, in 1703, the town of Boston took salary matters into its hands again, and retained them for the most part through the entire century.[3]

It is perfectly clear, upon the other hand, that a comparatively large number of towns did fix the method of payment through the town meeting during much of the late seventeenth and early eighteenth centuries. Braintree, at its public town meeting in 1668, determined that the school should be supported partly by the parents of children and partly by the town. It consented "to lay the Schoole land," that is to say, the annual income of it, for "a salliry for a Schoolemaster, and to make it up twenty pound besides what every child must give."[4] In 1716 the town again assumed to fix the method of school support. It established a school at the "south end" of the town, "to be at the charge of ye Town."[5] Watertown, in 1667, allotted the sum of thirty pounds for the schoolmaster, and the "towne agreed that the Schoole should be Free to all the setteled Inhabitance: Children that thir Freinds liue in other townes; to pay as before: & their payment to be deducted out of the 30 L; and the remaynder to be made vp by Rate."[6] Plymouth town meeting, in 1699, set the rates that should be charged the parents of children, and decreed that "what shall Remain due to sd scole to be Levied by Rate on the whole Inhabitants."[7] The payment of the school is again provided for in a specific manner in 1703/4 and 1705.[8] Muddyriver, which later became the town of Brookline, at a general meeting held in 1705 voted twelve pounds for a school, the rest to be raised on the heads of children.[9] Springfield, through its town meeting, rated all the

[1] Boston, *Rep. Rec. Com.*, vii., 161.

[2] *Ibid.*, ii., 125 *et seq.;* vii., 22 *et seq.*

[3] *Ibid.*, viii., 22 *et seq.;* xii., 4 *et seq.;* xiv., xvi., xviii., xxvi., xxxi.

[4] Braintree, *Records*, p. 9.

[5] *Ibid.*, p. 88.

[6] Watertown, *Records*, p. 91.

[7] Plymouth, *Records*, i., 270.

[8] *Ibid.*, i., 319; ii., 1.

[9] Brookline, *Records*, i., 90.

children "in the Town plat," between the years of five and ten, for the support of the school. This was in 1692.[1] In 1706/7 the town meeting refused to abolish the charge on scholars, indicating that the town as a whole settled these questions.[2] In 1708 the town agreed to pay the charge for schools beyond what was paid by the children.[3] Further instances might be cited throughout the first half of the century. Lancaster, in 1718, allowed the schoolmaster forty pounds, and agreed to "Raise the same by the Next Invoice."[4] Tisbury town meeting, in 1738, voted sixty-five pounds to "be raised upon the ratable Polls & Ratable Estates &c of the Inhabitants."[5]

Thus far the General Court had passed two laws giving some power in educational matters to the selectmen of the towns. The law of 1642 had given them supervision over education of children in the family, though not over education in the school. And the supervision was exercised. The law of 1647 had given them the power to decide how the salary of the elementary teacher, at least, should be paid; by the parents of school children, or by the town as a whole. And this authority seems not to have been exercised by them to any noticeable extent, the town generally making decisions upon such matters. Between the years 1647 and 1789 the General Court passed four measures which tended to give to the selectmen an increased power in school affairs. Two of these acts had to do with the matter of certification of teachers. One tacitly assumed the joint responsibility of inhabitants and selectmen for the keeping of required schools. The other confirmed the power of the selectmen to assess property for school and other affairs.

The first of these laws was the law of May 3, 1654. It "doth therfore commend it to the serious consideration & speciall care of the . . . selectmen in the seuerall townes, not to admitt or suffer any such to be contynued in the office or place of teaching, educating or instructing of youth or child, in the . . . schooles, that haue manifested y^m^selves vnsound in the fayth, or scandelous in theire liues, & not giueing due satisfaction according to the rules of Christ."[6]

This act evidently intended to have the selectmen exercise

1 Springfield, *Records*, ii., 205.
2 *Ibid.*, ii. 373.
3 *Ibid.*, ii., 380.
4 Lancaster, *Records*, p. 185.
5 Tisbury, *Records*, p. 106.
6 *Records of Mass.*, iii., 343, 344

some special supervision over the moral and religious character of the teachers. It evidently applied to teachers of all schools, elementary as well as secondary, as the phrase "instructing of youth or child" is used. It was not in any sense compulsory, as the General Court "doth commend it" merely. The mere fact that compulsory laws on certification were passed later, in 1701/2 [1] and 1711/2,[2] bears out the interpretation, as the merely commendatory act apparently proved insufficient for the purposes of the central government, which passed these more detailed and stringent laws.

There is little evidence that the selectmen had exercised any large amount of control over the selection of teachers up to this time, consequently little certificating power. Outside of the few towns mentioned below, there is little record in most of the towns that the selectmen had anything to do with the teacher prior to 1654. In Boston, in 1644 and 1645, the selectmen ordered certain amounts of money to the use of the schoolmaster.[3] In 1651 the town of Dorchester voted that the selectmen and two others should "treate and agree with" a schoolmaster.[4] In 1649 the selectmen of Watertown conducted the correspondence with the master selected by the town.[5] In 1652/3 the Dedham selectmen agreed with a schoolmaster at a certified rate, and the same was approved by the town.[6] This constitutes the meagre record of the action of the selectmen of these towns during this period. It is not extensive, nor does it indicate that the selectmen exercised any particular care as to the qualifications of the teachers.

The selectmen's activities during this earlier period touched other school matters more, perhaps, than they did the schoolmaster. In 1639 the town's regulations for the school at Dorchester allowed the selectmen and the elders to decide whether girls should be taught in the school, and the selectmen were also to appoint "one" to collect the school moneys.[7] In 1645, if money is lacking for repairs, the selectmen are empowered "to taxe the Towne" for the requisite amount.[8] The Boston selectmen showed much activity in the management of the school

1 Mass., *Prov. Acts & Res.*, i., 470.
2 *Ibid.* i., 681, 682.
3 Boston, *Rep. Rec. Com.*, ii., 82, 86.
4 *Ibid.*, iv., 304.
5 Watertown, *Records*, p. 18.
6 Dedham, *Records*, i., 213.
7 Boston, *Rep. Rec. Com.*, iv., 39.
8 *Ibid.*, iv., 55.

lands, frequently under direct instruction from the town meeting. In 1647 the selectmen rented Deare Island. In 1649 they attended to the matter of binding the inhabitants of Long and Spectacle Islands to an annual rent.[1] Other financial matters, other than the care of lands, were delegated to the selectmen of Dedham. In 1658 the town decided to build a schoolhouse, "the care of which is left to the select men."[2] In 1651, subcommittees of the selectmen agreed with workmen for work on the schoolhouse.[3] In the same year money out of the "Meadfield Rate" was assigned for payment.[4] A year later the selectmen proposed specific rules for the financial management of the school, to be approved by the town.[5]

In the period following the commendatory act of 1654, the selectmen had far more to do with school affairs, particularly in the selection and hiring of the teacher. This fact suggests that the law of 1654 established a precedent in the matter of school control to a larger extent than it followed one. Such activities range from the mere payment of and agreement with a teacher to the actual selection and hiring of the teacher by the selectmen. As the various towns are studied there seems to be a distinct trend from the merely formal agreement with a teacher, after the town had made a selection, to the actual and more or less independent appointment of a schoolmaster directly by the selectmen.

This tendency towards the acquisition of increased powers in school affairs by the selectmen is shown more or less clearly in certain representative towns. The selectmen of Dorchester, in the period from 1655 to 1675, seem merely to have made the agreement with the schoolmasters for the town, with one exceptional instance.[6] In 1660 the town asked the selectmen "to p'vide a schol maister."[7] Later, in 1681 and 1683, they are clearly "empowered by the town to hire a school master."[8] These are the latest items in the printed volume of records.

[1] Boston, *Rep. Rec. Com.*, ii., 92, 94, 95, 97. [3] *Ibid.*, i., 182.
[2] Dedham, *Records*, i., 123. [4] *Ibid.*, i., 195. [5] *Ibid.*, i., 202.
[6] Boston, *Rep. Rec. Com.*, iv., 73, 108, 155, 159, 182, 188, 210.
[7] *Ibid.*, iv., 166. In 1673/4, the town voted that there be "a Schoole Master p'cuered as formerly" and that "the Select men doe take care therein." (*Ibid.*, iv., 198). It is not clear, however, that the town gave over the election of a master. [8] *Ibid.*, iv., 257, 268.

In the period just prior to 1689, the Boston selectmen, by gradually established precedent and by instructions of the town meeting, dealt with most of the school business of the town.[1] In that year a vote of the town restored "the former Custome & practice in managing the affaires of the free schools" to the town in larger part.[2] But the selectmen still arranged many matters touching the affairs of the schoolmaster. In 1689/90 the town hired a schoolmaster and ordered that the "Select men agree with him."[3] In 1693 the selectmen were arranging the details of Ezekiel Cheever's recompense.[4] In 1699 they were making an agreement with Cheever's assistant.[5] The change of policy seems to have begun with the year 1700. In that year the town gave permission for the establishment of three schools for young children, and stipulated that the selectmen provide the schoolmasters.[6] In 1703 they were again instructed to "take care to procure Some meet person to be an assistant to Mr Ezekiell Chever."[7] In 1711/2, the consideration "of a proper person for a School master" was again given over to the selectmen, and they were "to Treat about Terms" with him.[8] From this time on and until 1788, the selectmen, either alone in part, or in company with others, selected and agreed with the teacher.[9]

Watertown presented the same tendency. The town elected the schoolmaster each year from 1650 to 1673.[10] In 1674, 1676, and 1677 the selectmen had charge of making the agreement with the teacher.[11] In 1678 the selectmen dismissed two teachers and selected another.[12] In 1678/9 the selectmen added to the agreement that they had made in 1678 by hiring the teacher for the complete year, instead of for part of the year.[13] The town vote of 1679 indicates that the town had, for the year at least,

[1] Boston, *Rep. Rec. Com.*, vii., 22 *et seq.*

[2] *Ibid.*, vii., 197.

[3] *Ibid.*, vii., 200.

[4] *Ibid.*, vii., 215.

[5] *Ibid.*, vii., 236, 238.

[6] *Ibid.*, vii., 240.

[7] *Ibid.*, viii., 28.

[8] *Ibid.*, viii., 90.

[9] *Ibid.*, vii., 93, 136, 137, 204; xii., 4, 13; xvi., 284; xviii., 252; xxxi., 17, 60. About the years 1719 and 1720 the town seems to have elected its masters instead of leaving such selection to the selectmen. This reversion in method seems not to have persisted. (*Ibid.*, viii., 139–143).

[10] Watertown, *Records*, p. 21 *et seq.*

[11] *Ibid.*, 127, 129.

[12] *Ibid.*, p. 137.

[13] *Ibid.*, p. 138.

resumed its former practice of electing a teacher at town meeting, but the tendency prior to this vote is clear.[1]

In Springfield the contact of the selectmen with matters relating to the school teacher began with agreements in behalf of the town. Later, the teacher is actually hired by the town's representatives. In 1683 the town requested its officers to arrange a stipend for the master then teaching, in order that he continue.[2] In 1685 there was another indenture made.[3] It was the same in 1686.[4] But in 1690 the selectmen were asked to "use their diligent care to provide a Schoolmaster" as well as "to agree with him." [5] This precedent is largely followed in 1708, 1716, and 1718.[6]

The same tendency appeared somewhat later in Brookline. The preliminary period, or rather the transitional period, where the selectmen merely make the agreement with teachers, is not at all well marked in this town. There are records of such agreements with the teacher in 1711 and 1718, however.[7] In 1746 there was an isolated case where the selectmen "provide a School Master." [8] The continuous movement in this direction commenced about 1783, when it was voted "that the Selectmen be directed to Ingage a Schoolmaster to keep School." [9] This is the only method of getting a teacher noted until after 1805,[10] when the school committees attended to the hiring of teachers.[11]

Other towns recorded, in a more isolated way, the tendency to delegate to the selectmen the procuring of a teacher. Duxbury, in 1730/1, recorded that its selectmen hired the teacher.[12] Oxford, in 1740, was provided with a schoolmaster by the selectmen.[13] Cambridge, as early as 1691, recorded that the "selectmen in behalf of ye Town . . . Called Sir Hancock to keep scoole for the Town." [14]

Neither Dedham nor Braintree show as complete an evolution in the matter of bestowing power with regard to the schoolmaster upon the selectmen as the towns above mentioned. The Dedham records show a strong and persistent custom of having

[1] Watertown, *Records*, p. 144.
[2] Springfield, *Records*, ii., 163, 164.
[3] *Ibid.*, ii., 173.
[4] *Ibid.*, ii., 194.
[5] *Ibid.*, ii. 200.
[6] *Ibid.*, ii., 380, 400, 404.
[7] Brookline, *Records*, i., 97,113,114.
[8] *Ibid.*, i., 160.
[9] *Ibid.*, i., 325.
[10] *Ibid.*, i., 357, 388, 463, 464.
[11] *Ibid.*, i., 488 *et seq.*
[12] Duxbury, *Records*, p. 242.
[13] Oxford, *Records*, p. 308.
[14] Cambridge, *Records*, p. 293.

the selectmen agree with the master after the town has selected him. This movement began as early as 1656 and extended up to the close of the printed records in 1673,[1] at which time the school committee movement had not manifested itself to a considerable degree in this particular town.

In the case of Braintree it was somewhat different. From 1682/3 till 1715 there was a repetition of agreements between the selectmen and the schoolmaster, who was usually chosen by the town.[2] Some slight tendency to let the selectmen actually hire the teacher appeared in two votes of the town. In 1700 the selectmen were instructed to agree with a Mr. Eells, "or if he refuse some other," implying some discretion in case the appointee of the town could not be obtained.[3] In 1708 they were to "provide a Gramer school Master" at a salary not above thirty pounds.[4] There is no established procedure of obtaining a teacher indicated in the town records after 1715, though they extend to 1792.[5]

The acquisition by the selectmen of authority to perform functions which had to do with the appointment of the teacher, while most important, was not the only development during this period. From the beginning there had been a tendency, already partly suggested, toward allowing the selectmen to handle the financial business of the town as related to the school, *i. e.*, to manage the school lands, to see that the rental of same was paid, to supervise the repair and erection of schoolhouses, and finally to assess for school needs under the supervision of the town meeting. Occasionally the selectmen exercised a watchful eye over the general management of the schools, perhaps even visited them, and made recommendations as to their proper conduct.

It was quite natural that the town should come to depend upon its selectmen for the detailed management of its financial affairs. The selectmen were in one sense the executive officers of the town, as the town meeting was its legislative branch. So we find that an important town such as Boston made considerable use of its selectmen in the management of the financial affairs of the schools. The management of the school lands,

[1] Dedham, *Records*, i., 140 *et seq.;* ii., 2 *et seq.*

[2] Braintree, *Records*, pp. 21, 41, 47, 51, 53, 58, 86.

[3] *Ibid.*, p. 47. [4] *Ibid.*, p. 69. [5] *Ibid.*, p. 123 *et seq.*

which was noticed in the study of the period prior to 1654, continued through the remainder of that century.[1] The sale and purchase of school lands remained a matter for the attention of the selectmen in the next century.[2] If a new schoolhouse were to be erected or an old one enlarged or repaired, all of which actions involved some expenditure of town funds, the selectmen were given the care of the matter. In 1657 the selectmen ordered the "house belonging to the schoole" repaired.[3] In 1664 two of the selectmen were ordered to care for the "inlardgment of the Towne school-house."[4] And there are many other instances extending through the succeeding decades.[5]

The other towns of Massachusetts utilized their selectmen in a similar fashion. A few cases will suggest the extent of the custom. In 1669 Cambridge, through its selectmen, agreed with workmen to tear down the schoolhouse and set it up again.[6] In the same year the selectmen voted forty shillings for the repairing of the schoolmaster's house.[7] The year following, the selectmen sold land to repair the schoolhouse.[8] Throughout the seventeenth century Dedham recorded the acts of its selectmen in paying the schoolmaster, in managing the levy and collection of the rate, and in ordering repairs.[9] The Dorchester selectmen during the same period attended to the school property, appointing committees to provide a lock, or repair a school building; regulated the school rate and the gathering of the same; and provided a method for supplying fuel to the school.[10] In Springfield the selectmen located the school, divided the school money, and assessed parents for the failure of their children to furnish school wood.[11] Braintree, in the later decades of the seventeenth century and during the beginning of the next century, recorded its selectmen as performing a large range of duties

[1] Boston, *Rep. Rec. Com.*, ii., 129, 130, 133, 140 *et seq.;* vii., 22 *et seq.*
[2] *Ibid.*, viii., 76, 77, 103 *et seq.*
[3] *Ibid.*, ii., 142.
[4] *Ibid.*, vii., 24.
[5] *Ibid.*, vii., 226, 244; viii., 8, 76, 77, 94, 110, 118, 119.
[6] Cambridge, *Records*, p. 180.
[7] *Ibid.*, p. 182.
[8] *Ibid.*, pp. 328, 330, 331, 334, 335.
[9] Dedham, *Records*, ii., 26, 27, 72, 91, 112, 123, 140 *et seq.*
[10] Boston, *Records*, iv., 96, 97, 151, 210, 223, 236, 267.
[11] Springfield, *Records*, ii., 143, 368, 380, 381.

involving some financial responsibility of the town, outside the matter of hiring a school teacher. The selectmen rented school lands, let the schoolhouse, attended to the erection and repair of schoolhouses, removed the school building, levied and abated school rates, etc.[1] Other towns, too numerous to mention, recorded acts of the same type.

This extension of the function of the selectmen in both the financial and the more purely educational aspects of school management and maintenance naturally led to a further recognition of the function of the selectmen by the General Court. In 1692/3 two acts of significance were passed. One empowered the selectmen to assess for schools and other purposes when so instructed by a majority vote of the inhabitants.[2] As has been shown, the selectmen had been attending to the financial details of school management. This law legalized such practice in one particular direction.

The other law laid certain requirements upon towns for the maintenance of schools of elementary and secondary type, and one particular portion reads: "And the selectmen and the inhabitants of such towns, respectively, shall take effectual care and make due provision for the settlement and maintenance of such school-master and masters."[3] This sentence in the law is a distinct incorporation of prevailing practice. The law laid the responsibility for the "settlement and maintenance" of schoolmasters upon the selectmen as well as upon the inhabitants in general. To a large extent this was a responsibility which had been delegated to or assumed by the selectmen. This law may then be regarded as an incorporation of current methods of school management.

The last of the four colonial laws concerning selectmen and the schools, passed subsequent to the act of 1647, is the act of 1711/2.[4] Of the four laws mentioned, it is in reality the first to confer power upon the selectmen as independent of the town. It gave to the selectmen, with reference to the elementary teacher, what the law of 1654 had merely commended to them with reference to both elementary and secondary teachers. In 1701/2 an act of the General Court had taken from the

[1] Braintree, *Records*, pp. 21, 33, 34, 36, 40, 50–52, 54, 82, 98, 118.

[2] Mass., *Prov. Acts & Res.*, i., 66.

[3] *Ibid.*, i., 63.

[4] Mass., *Prov. Acts & Res.*, i., 681, 682.

selectmen the power to certificate secondary teachers by definitely giving this power to the ministers.[1] The law of 1711/2 now gave the power of certificating elementary teachers definitely to the selectmen. This law provided as follows:

> That no person or persons shall or may presume to set up or keep a school for the teaching and instructing of children or youth in reading, writing, or any other science, but such as are of sober conversation, and have the allowance and approbation of the selectmen of the town in which any such school is to be kept. [2]

The tendency of the town-meeting to delegate its powers to other representatives of the town has been indicated. The tendency of the town to delegate a large part of its school business to the selectmen has been partially indicated. The movement toward giving the ministers some power in school affairs was suggested by a mention of the law of 1701/2. There is still another authority, the fuller development of which is to be traced later, which in the eighteenth century became of such importance as to share the main responsibility for school supervision along with the selectmen and the ministers, and which was destined finally to overshadow them both. This was the school committee. The power of the selectmen tended to decline as the school committee was given increased power, (1) by the towns which used special school committees instead of the selectmen; and (2) by the General Court, which recognized the school committee as an institution for educational affairs, and later employed it as the main channel for school control.

It was the law of 1789[3] which first recognized in a single act the relative place of town and district selectmen, minister, and school committee in educational control and supervision. Up to this time it cannot be truly said that the rise of the minister or the school committee had shorn the selectmen of much of their power, for the newer agencies had risen to meet the newer demands of school evolution. The law of 1789 represented the highest power of the minister and selectmen in school affairs. After that law, however, the educational authority of each declined, and the school committee rose to become the main agency for educational work.

[1] Mass., *Prov. Acts & Res.*, i., 470.

[2] *Ibid.*, i., 681, 682.

[3] *Acts of 1789*, chap. xix. (Mass., *Perpetual Laws*, ii., 39–44).

This law gave the selectmen a distinctly additional power connected with the classification and grading of schools. Grammar schools, according to the state law, were to admit only those able "to read the English language, by spelling the same," but the selectmen of the town were given the power, at their discretion, to "direct the grammar schoolmaster to receive and instruct such." [1] Thus it lay within the power of the selectmen to change a secondary school into a combination elementary and secondary school.

More important than the right to determine the grade of schools was the imposition of the duty of visitation and inspection of schools upon the selectmen conjointly with the minister or ministers of the town. The same section of the law likewise made it the duty of ministers and selectmen "to use their influence and best endeavours" that the youth of the town attend the schools. The portion of the law reads as follows:

> . . . And it shall be the duty of the minister or ministers of the gospel and the Selectmen (or such other persons as shall be specially chosen by each town or district for that purpose,) of the several towns or districts, to use their influence and best endeavours, that the youth of their respective towns and districts do regularly attend the schools appointed and supported as aforesaid, for their instruction; and once in every six months at least, and as much oftener as they shall determine it necessary, to visit and inspect the several schools in their respective towns and districts, and shall inquire into the regulation and discipline thereof, and the proficiency of the scholars therein, giving reasonable notice of the time of their visitation. [2]

The growing custom of having the selectmen hire the schoolmaster was now legalized by the act of 1789. The authorization was incidental rather than explicit, and occurred in connection with the section on the certification of teachers resident in the town where the school was to be kept. The law reads: "It shall however be the duty of such Selectmen or Committee, who may be authorized to hire such schoolmaster, specially to attend to his morals." [3] It will be noticed that the selectmen or school committee are not empowered to hire the teacher save upon being specially authorized by the town or district.

The function of certification was recognized as a proper one

[1] *Acts of 1789*, chap. xix. sec. 3 (Mass., *Perpetual Laws*, ii., 40).
[2] *Acts of 1789*, chap. xix., sec. 8 (Mass., *Perpetual Laws*, ii., 42, 43).
[3] *Acts of 1789*, chap. xix., sec. 6 (Mass., *Perpetual Laws*, ii, 41).

for detailed treatment in the law, and definite standards and methods of certification of teachers both as to educational and moral fitness are laid down. Considerable shifting in the matter of responsibility for certification occurred with the passing of this law. Before this time, the ministers were responsible for both educational and moral qualifications of secondary teachers[1]; and the selectmen for both qualifications of the elementary teacher.[2] Now the selectmen of the town where the candidates for the position of "instructors of youth" resided might certify as to their moral character.[3] This was an increase of the selectmen's power. The former law merely permitted them to certificate elementary teachers.

There was a tendency to curtail the power of the selectmen in the certification of elementary teachers. Where, before, the selectmen had held this power exclusively, the law now required, in addition, a certificate "from a learned minister settled" in the town where the school was to have been kept, "if such there be," thus dividing in certain cases the selectmen's power with the "learned minister . . . if such there be."[4]

But there was a more important tendency toward the curtailing of the selectmen's power which appeared throughout this act; more important because of its ultimate consequences. Though the act of 1789 tended on the whole to increase, by specific reference of function, the power of the selectmen, it likewise recognized another official body which was permitted to perform the functions of certification, visitation, and the enforcement of school attendance in lieu of the selectmen. This official body is the committee for school purposes which the town may have appointed. Wherever the selectmen were mentioned in connection with the above-named functions, the school committee of the town, if there was one, was likewise given the same power. It is "the selection of such town or district, or committee of such parish or place."[5] It is "such Selectmen or Committee, who may be authorized to hire such schoolmaster."[6] It is "the

[1] Mass., *Prov. Acts & Res.*, i., 470.

[2] *Ibid.*, i., 681, 682.

[3] *Acts of 1789*, chap. xix., secs. 4, 5 (Mass., *Perpetual Laws*, ii., 40, 41).

[4] *Ibid.*, sec. 10 (Mass., *Perpetual Laws*, ii., 43).

[5] *Acts of 1789*, chap. xix., sec. 5 (Mass., *Perpetual Laws*, ii., 41).

[6] *Acts of 1789*, chap. xix., sec. 6 (Mass. *Perpetual Laws* ii., 41).

Selectmen (or such other persons as shall be specially chosen by each town or district for that purpose).[1] And it is "the Selectmen of such town or district where the same [school] may be kept, or the committee appointed by such town, district, or plantation to visit their school." [2]

While there was this tendency to restrict the authority of selectmen upon school matters, it is to be noted that it was in such purely educational matters as the certification and hiring of teachers and the visitation and inspection of schools, powers which were permitted to existing school committees instead. In other matters, more strictly concerning the administrative management of the schools, the tendency is somewhat the opposite. This opposite tendency is further confirmed by an act passed in 1800, which gave the selectmen the additional power of locating district schoolhouses when the people of the district were unable to agree.[3]

Nor must it be assumed that the giving of power to the school committees at once stripped the selectmen of power in even such matters as certification, inspection, and other such functions. The committees in some cases included the selectmen as members. The committee appointed by Boston on the reorganization of its schools in 1789 consisted "of twelve in addition to the Selectmen." [4]

With the law of 1826, requiring the establishment of school committees in the towns, the power of the selectmen as a distinct official body having control of certification of teachers and the visitation and inspection of schools came to an end, for these powers were hereafter vested in the school committee.[5] The law of 1827 reaffirmed the provisions of the act of 1826 and established the prudential committee-man in each school district, giving him the power "to select and contract with a school teacher for his own district." [6] Thus the last of the powers concerning the teacher and his work had passed from the selectmen to the school committees.

[1] *Acts of 1789*, chap. xix., sec. 8 (Mass. *Perpetual Laws*, ii., 42).

[2] *Acts of 1789*, chap. xix., sec. 10 (Mass. *Perpetual Laws*, ii., 43).

[3] Mass., *Perpetual Laws*, ii., 80.

[4] Boston, *Rep. Rec. Com.*, xxxi., 209.

[5] Mass., *Acts of 1826*, chap. clxx. (pp. 299–303.)

[6] Mass., *Acts of 1827*, chap. cxliii. (pp. 557–572.)

The act of 1827 marked the final passing of the town selectmen as an official body for conducting school affairs. The burden of the general care and management of the schools had become too heavy a burden to be carried along with all the other business of the town. As the earlier town meeting had given over many of its school duties to the selectmen, the selectmen, in turn, now gave over their special responsibility to the specialized agencies which it had taken almost two centuries to evolve —the school committee of the town and the prudential committee of the district.

The selectmen had gathered power in school affairs very slowly, as slowly as the various powers developed as distinct functions. The precedent was laid in that act of 1642, when the selectmen were given the supervision of education in the home. Gradually the town gave them much of the detail of managing matters which had to do with the financial support of the school, matters of school administration in the broad sense which persisted in their hands to the nineteenth century. Then the business side of hiring the teacher fell to their lot, and a long record of agreements with the teacher in behalf of the town preceded the records of the actual selecting and hiring of the teachers. From the middle of the seventeenth century, through the middle of the succeeding century, the selectmen were relatively most important in managing school affairs. Then the school committee came into prominence and shared the power of supervising the educational affairs of the school. By the end of the century, in 1789, they divided the privileges and duties. In 1827 the school committees assumed the control of the internal management of the school, and the period of delegation of school powers to the selectmen was over.

CHAPTER IV

THE MINISTER AND OTHERS IN SCHOOL AFFAIRS

In three succeeding periods in the history of education in Massachusetts, the details of school affairs were predominantly handled by three distinct bodies in turn. In the very earliest period the town meeting attended to the necessities of the school. Then, as matters became more complicated, the busi-

was delegated to the selectmen, the town's representatives in settling such exigencies as might arise between sessions of the inhabitants. Later, the school committee, designed primarily for school affairs, became the important instrument in school management. But the evolution of school supervision from town to committee did not occur without some groping after means before the school committee was finally seized as the fit instrument.

There were a number of tendencies toward the utilization of various officers of the town in school affairs. It seems a natural tendency for a community to attempt to use officials and official bodies already in existence for their purposes, before finally devising some newer method of caring for the town's interests. This accounts for the use of the selectmen in such large part. There were other agencies which are mentioned in the school records of the Massachusetts towns. But save for the use of the minister, they are, for the most part, rather more interesting than significant. They may be merely noted in passing. They are not found in many of the town records. For the most part they are limited to Boston and a few other towns.

It is rather strange to think of the town constables in school affairs. And they did not play any very important part. As the custodians of the town money and the collectors of the school rates, they are mentioned somewhat in matters which have to do with the school money. The Boston selectmen ordered the constables to pay the schoolmaster's salary in 1664.[1] In 1645 the constables were ordered by the same authority to set aside money "for mending the Schoole Master his part of the partition fence."[2] Watertown, in 1655, recorded the delivery into the hands of the constables of "a rate For the cuntery and the Colledg."[3] Braintree, much later, in 1695/6, recorded the acknowledgment by the schoolmaster of money received from the town constables.[4] But such records might be expected. They are no more strange than the payment and receipt of town moneys by the modern town treasurer. A record which is more unusual is that found in the Cambridge Records in 1656, when "The Townsmen do agree that the Constables do forth with take effectuall care for the repaire of the meeting house, and the

[1] Boston, *Rep. Rec. Com.*, ii., 82.

[2] *Ibid.*, ii., 86.

[3] Watertown, *Records*, p. 42.

[4] Braintree, *Records*, p. 33.

schoole house."[1] It is an isolated instance, however. In most cases, as has been shown, such matters would have been attended to, at this period, by the selectmen.

The action of the justices in school matters, where such was recorded, is somewhat peculiar. In general, with the constables they were vested with the enforcement of the laws relating to schools.[2] But this was a legal matter. There are some instances where matters more intimately connected with the settlement and maintenance of schools were given to the justices either alone or with others. When "the president and Council of his Majesties Territory and dominion" gave the inhabitants of Muddyriver (later the town of Brookline) permission to have a school of their own apart from Boston, it was decreed "that within one year next Coming thay raise a school House in such place as the Two next Justices of the Countie upon a publick hearing of the Inhabitants of the sd Hamlet shall Determine."[3] The Boston records show that "It was then ordered by sd Justices & Selectmen. That the School house lately Built in the Prison lane . . . Remaine as it is now fenced in." This was in 1698.[4]

It has been suggested that most of the instances of the peculiar use of town officials other than selectmen and ministers are to be found in Boston. In several places mention is to be found of the use of committees or Overseers of the Poor in connection with the management of schools. This is not to be wondered at, when it is remembered that "learning and labor" were coupled in that law of 1642, which was seemingly a colonial adaptation of the old English poor laws.[5] In 1678/9 the proposition for "A Free Schoole to teach the Children of poore people" was referred to the selectmen.[6] Later, in 1682, the committee of five on "Almes and work house" were, with the

[1] Cambridge, *Records*, p. 112.

[2] *Records of Mass.*, iv., pt. 2, 396; also see Mass., *Prov. Acts & Resolves*, i., 470.

[3] Brookline, *Records*, i., 85, 86.

[4] Boston, *Rep. Rec. Com.*, vii., 233.

[5] *Records of Mass.*, ii., 6, 7. Cf. *Act 6, Anne, cap. 46*, Nicholls, *History of the English Poor Laws*, i., 367. This seems to be a similar though later development in England, embodying somewhat the same ideas as those included in the Act of 1642.

[6] Boston, *Rep. Rec. Com.*, vii., 127.

selectmen, appointed to "consider of & pvide one or more Free Schooles for the teachinge of Children to write & Cypher within this towne."[1] In 1683 the committee reported in favor of the establishment of two schools.[2] So, in this instance, the connection of a committee on the affairs of the poor with schools "to teach the Children of poore people" is somewhat easily understood. These schools had to do with the "learning" side of that demand of the commonwealth, expressed in the law of 1642. In 1720 the town of Boston proceeded to take some action on the "labor" side of that demand. This action provided for "the choyce of a Committee to Consider abt promoting of a Spinning School or Schools."[3] In 1755 the twelve "The Gentlemen The Overseers of the Poor" are recorded as a portion of the committee, which with the selectmen made the annual visitation and inspection of the Boston schools.[4] This visitation of these Overseers of the Poor evidently continued each year thereafter.[5] In 1769 spinning schools for the poor were actually set up.[6] In 1784 a "Comittee appointed to consider of a future Arangment of the free Schools In this Town," reported and recommended that the Overseers of the Poor provide instruction in the fundamentals to the poor, both boys and girls.[7] It was not long before the conception of free schools for all as a necessity to the republic became current and free education as related to pauperism was less likely to be conspicuous.

In connection with this same committee of visitation, of which the Overseers of the Poor were a part, it is interesting to notice that, in 1751, "the Gentlemen the Representatives of Boston" appeared. They continued to be recorded among the committee for many years.[8] The function of the Overseers and Representatives of the commonwealth was, to a large extent, formal. The work of visitation, with Governor and Lieutenant-Governor frequent members of a committee, which sometimes reached a total of thirty-eight, not including the Overseers,

[1] Boston, *Rep. Rec. Com.*, vii., 158.

[2] *Ibid.*, vii., 161.

[3] *Ibid.*, viii., 147, 148.

[4] *Ibid.*, xiv., 275, 276.

[5] *Ibid.*, xiv., 308, 309; xvi., 10 11, 25, 26, 77, 78, 95, 96, 113–115, 141, 142, 180, 181, 245, 246, 284, 285; xviii., 24, 25, 54, 55, 78, 79, 129–131.

[6] *Ibid.*, xvi., 275–277.

[7] *Ibid.*, xxxi., 18.

[8] *Ibid.*, xiv., 195 *et seq.;* xvi., 10 *et seq.;* xviii., 24 *et seq.*

Representatives, and selectmen, [1] could not have been very serious and efficient educational inspection.

There was a tendency, however, to confer some power on the religious officers of the town, which was far more important than any of the above-mentioned instances. The leaders of the colony of Massachusetts Bay "were fully agreed, that the main object of the colony should be to uphold the Puritan faith and to form a society in harmony therewith." [2] It is little to be wondered at that the religious officers of the community were frequently called into service upon school affairs, particularly when education was a necessary part of the Puritan belief. The early records frequently mention the deacons and elders of the churches as members of school committees appointed for various purposes.

When Dorchester appointed its first wardens of the town school, in 1645, Deacon Wiswall was one among the three named.[3] In 1651 this same Deacon Wiswall, along with a Mr. Jones, did "treate and Agree" with a schoolmaster.[4] Again, in 1681, the Dorchester selectmen appointed two of their number "to enquier after a Schole Mr." and one of them was a Deacon Blake.[5] In 1684 the Boston selectmen appointed two of their number to agree with a teacher, and one of the appointees was "Deacon Henery Allen." [6] Deacon Nathaniel Wales was one of the five men "chosen to erect & finnish a new Schoole House" in Braintree in 1699.[7] The same town listed "Dean Thomas Wales on a committee of three "to examine into the state of the school."[8] Cambridge, in 1700, through its selectmen, appointed Deacon Hastings, along with a John Leverett, to contract for the "Rebuilding the Schoolhouse." [9] In 1777 Deacon Joseph White resigned from the School Committee of Brookline.[10] There were many other instances where deacons of the church were found actively engaged in school affairs.

The mention of elders in school affairs of the early periods is less frequent than that of deacons. Dedham had, as one of its

1 Boston, *Rep. Rec. Com.*, xviii., 129–131.
2 Osgood, *American Colonies in the 17th Cent.*, i., 208.
3 Boston, *Rep. Rec. Com.*, iv., 45.
4 *Ibid.*, iv., 304.
5 *Ibid.*, iv., 256.
6 *Ibid.*, vii., 171.
7 Braintree, *Records*, p. 40.
8 *Ibid.*, p. 382.
9 Cambridge, *Records*, p. 331.
10 Brookline, *Records*, i., 264.

five "Feofeess" for the school, "Eldr Eliazer Lusher." This was in 1644. He was also a selectman at this time.[1] He was on a committee to parcel out the school land in this same year. In 1651 the same elder was on two more school committees for temporary purposes.[3] In 1680 the selectmen of Dorchester appointed "Elder Humphry to Cattechiz the youth and Children." [4] In none of these cases where deacons and elders are mentioned, is there any evidence to show that they were appointed because of their church office. They might have been appointed for other reasons. In two of these instances it is probable that they were appointed because they were selectmen, as the acts of appointment seem to be the appointment of sub-committees of the selectmen.

There are a number of instances, however, where educational matters were left in the hands of the elders as officials. The conferring of power seems to have been upon the office instead of upon individual persons, who might have merely happened to be elders. When Dorchester drew up its first school regulations, in 1639, the town ordered "that it is left to the discretion of elders and the 7 men for the tyme beeing whether maydes shalbe taught with the boyes or not." [5] The records of the Free School in Roxburie for the year 1668 include the following sentence, which is of a similar nature: "The Lord having taken away two of the Feoffees by death, by the liberty of the rest the Feoffees have they have compleated their number by the choice of our two Elders." [6] In 1683 there was a similar use of the elders in the school affairs of Dedham. Certain money had been given by a Doctor Wm. Avery for the use of a Latin school, and the care of the same was placed in the hands of a committee of three, who "are desired and impowered wth the Revd elders and Select men to take care of and to dispose of the money aboue saide as it may be secured and improued for the end mentioned." [7]

The mention of ministers as members of committees on school affairs during the seventeenth century was even less frequent than that of the elders. Such mention is found in the

[1] Dedham, *Records*, i., 104, 105.
[2] *Ibid.*, i., 108.
[3] *Ibid.*, i., 182, 192, 193.
[4] Boston, *Rep. Rec. Com.*, iv., 255.
[5] *Ibid.*, iv., 39.
[6] Dillaway, *op. cit.*, p. 29.
[7] Dedham, *Historical Register*, ii., 7.

case of Dorchester in 1666, when "Master Mather" is one of three to get a teacher.[1] In 1669, William Stoughton, who frequently acted as minister, was on a similar committee.[2] Minister Stoughton was also a selectman at this time.[3] Just how far the ministers actually occupied official positions on committees for school affairs, is not evident. Recalling that the ministers represented the learned class, it would be expected that committees on schoolmasters might include the minister; but the records at hand show few cases. It would probably be incorrect to measure the influence of the minister in the school affairs of the New England theocracy by his absence from, or his presence on, school committees which were temporary in their purposes. The influence of the ministerial office alone might have been considerable.

The first recognition of the ministers in the management of school affairs by the colonial government came at the very beginning of the eighteenth century, when a law placed the certification of grammar-school masters in the hands of the ministers. This law of June 25, 1701/2, reads: "Every grammar-school master [is] to be approved by the minister of the town, and the ministers of the next two adjacent towns, or any two of them, by certificate under their hands." [4] This obligation was reasserted in the Act of 1711/2.[5]

In a general way, the selectmen in 1654 had been requested to care for the religious and moral character of school masters. Just what was behind the definite delegation of the certification of grammar-school masters, it is difficult to say. Evidently the framers of the law felt the necessity of controlling those who might teach in the secondary schools and expressed it through this act. The secondary schools were probably of greater concern to the people of this time than the elementary schools, which had not yet attained the recognition that was to come in the early nineteenth century.

It is easier to understand why this power was given to the ministers rather than to the selectmen or any other officials. Such certification involved two things: academic training and moral or religious fitness. In the seventeenth century, which

[1] Dedham, *Historial Register*, iv., 136, 145.

[2] *Ibid.*, iv., 159.

[3] *Ibid.*, iv., 182.

[4] Mass., *Prov. Acts & Res.*, i., 470.

[5] *Ibid.*, i., 681, 682.

had just expired before the enactment of this law, "The ministry was the only learned or professional class then in New England."[1] In those days "The college and the grammar school . . . were parts of one educational system. . . . In both alike the ideal of education was an ideal of public service. . . . And the form of public service which was uppermost in the minds of their founders, was the Christian ministry."[2] Consequently, because the ministers were the only ones fitted as a group to judge of the learning of teachers, they were made the certificating power. Then the preservation of a learned ministry demanded learned teachers in grammar school and college, and the learned ministers were themselves best fitted to uphold the traditions of their own calling. Again, since there was an important judgment to be made upon moral and religious fitness as laid down in the law of 1654, the ministers were by far the best judges as to those "that haue manifested ymselves vnsound in the fayth, or scandelous in theire liues, & not giueing due satisfaction according to the rules of Christ."[3] Who would know the rules of Christ better than the Christian ministers? If the selectmen had failed, was it not time to place the authority where it properly belonged? The conferring of the certificating power on the ministers seemed the one natural thing.

Beside the logic of the situation there was ample precedent. In 1631[4] the religious test for citizenship had been applied, and that test required that "henceforth no man shall be admitted to the freedome of this Commonwealth, but such as are members of some of the Churches, within the limits of this Iurisdiction."[5] Those best fitted to certify to this religious test were the ministers. When the law of 1664 amended the requirement in a somewhat ambiguous way, it stated clearly one point; "that from henceforth all Englishmen must present" a Certificate under the hand of the Ministers, or Minister of the Place where they dwell."[6] The law of 1701/2 applied to grammar-school teachers what the law of 1664 had applied to freemen of the Commonwealth.

[1] Osgood, *Amer. Colonies in the 17th Century*, i., 208.

[2] Brown, *Making of our Middle Schools*, p. 57.

[3] *Records of Mass.*, iii., 244, 343.

[4] Osgood, *American Colonies in the 17th Century*, i., 212.

[5] Whitmore, *Colonial Laws*, i., 153.

[6] *Ibid.*, i., 3.

While one section of this act had conferred educational power upon the minister, another had made a discrimination against him. Section three of this act states "That no minister of any town be deemed, held, or accepted to be the schoolmaster of such town within the intent of the law."[1] The placing of this disability upon the "settled minister" was reaffirmed in the act of 1789.[2] It was not until June 26, 1811, that this disability was removed by an act of repeal.[3] This section was probably due to the fact that the law requiring grammar schools in certain towns was being avoided by the use of the settled minister as grammar teacher in certain communities.[4]

Beside this express power in the certification of grammar-school teachers given to the ministers by the General Court, there were, undoubtedly, other supervisory functions which were performed by the ministers. The extent of their actual influence will always be difficult of determination. Mr. Martin, in his discussion of the "Schools before the Revolution," lays great stress upon the activity of the minister in school supervision. He says that the schools "were under the constant and vigilant supervision of the ministers . . . he visited the schools regularly, frequently questioned the children on the sermon of the preceding Sunday, and periodically examined them in the catechism and in their knowledge of the Bible."[5] The town records of Boston show the statement to be true of Boston, from 1710 on, and there are certain statements made in the records which would lend authority to the opinion that the ministers had exercised some oversight in educational matters before that time. The records of other towns where there were annual school committees, as in Boston after 1710, do not show that ministers were members of these committees in the Colonial period.

The town of Boston, at a meeting of December 19, 1709, "Voted. That a Committee be chosen to consider of the affaires relateing to the Gram̃er Free School of this Town, and to make report thereof at the Town meeting in march next."[6] That

[1] Mass., *Prov. Acts & Res.*, i., 470.

[2] Mass., *Perpetual Laws*, ii., 41. (*Acts of 1789*, chap. xix., sec. 6.)

[3] Mass., *Public & General Laws*, iv., 268.

[4] Martin, *Evolution of the Mass. School System*, p. 70.

[5] *Ibid* p. 64.

[6] Boston, *Rep. Rec. Com.*, viii., 63.

committee in the formulation of its report, or before, consulted the ministers of the town. In their report presented to the town meeting in March of 1709/10, they expressly stated, at the close of a recommendation for increased assistance and recompense for the grammar-school master, that the recommendation was one "In which we have ye concurrent Opinion and Advice of ye Revrd Ministers." [1] It would then seem that the relationship of the ministers to the schools was such, in the particular case of Boston at least, as to warrant a distinguished committee consulting them.

Another portion of the report distinctly alluded to the existence of a precedent both in England and America. It reads as follows:

> We further propose and recommend, as of Great Service and Advantage for the promoting of Diligence and good literature, That the Town Agreeably to the Usage in England, and (as we understand) in Some time past practiced here, Do Nominate and Appoint a Certain Number of Gentlemen, of Liberal Education, Together with Some of ye Revd Ministers of the Town to be Inspectors of the Sd Schoole under that name Title or denomination, To Visit ye School from time to time, when and as Oft, as they shall thinck fit to Enform themselves of the methodes used in teaching of ye Schollars and to Inquire of their Proficiency, and be present at the performance of Some of their Exercises, the Master being before Notified of their Comeing, And with him to consult and Advise of further Methods for ye Advancement of Learning and the Good Government of the Schoole.
>
> And at their Sd Visitation, one of the ministers by turns to pray with the Schollars, and entertain 'em with Some Instructions of Piety Specially adapted to their age and Education. [2]

The town then chose a committee to act with the ministers, in accordance with the recommendation of the committee.[3] Mr. Martin is authority for the statement that "Increase Mather was highly incensed at the innovation, and after declaring that the ministers were the fittest persons in the world to be the visitors of the schools, pettishly declared that he would not go with the lay inspectors, but would go when he pleased, and would go alone." [4] If such a statement is authentic, it would confirm the belief that the ministers of Boston had been in the habit of actively supervising the schools.

[1] Boston, *Rep. Rec. Com.*, viii., 64, 65. [2] *Ibid.*, viii., 65. [3] *Ibid.*
[4] Martin, *Evolution of the Mass. Public School System*, p. 65.

Beside the function of visitation, the inspectors and ministers were, in 1709/10, given the authority to introduce an usher for the Latin school. They were to agree with him as to a just recompense for the future, as they were to agree with the old usher for his services.[1] In 1710/1, the five inspectors to act with the ministers were again elected, and a memorial, which the selectmen of the town had formulated in criticism of the methods and study of the Latin school, was referred to this joint committee of laymen and ministers for their consideration.[2] The records give no trace of any further election of this committee in the subsequent years. So that the particular practice of the town can not be determined definitely.

For about five years, beginning with 1713/4, "ye Sel:men together with the Reverend Ministers of this Town" were requested to act as inspectors of both grammar schools of the town. Here they divided, with the selectmen, the duty of visiting all the secondary schools of the town.[3]

In the year 1721 the committee of visitation was to visit all the schools of the town, writing schools as well as grammar schools. The composition of the committee of visitation was fixed by the town meeting, and was of "the Selectmen with Such others as they Shal take with them." [4] All the available detailed records of the persons invited by the selectmen would seem to show that the ministers were always included. In the succeeding decade, when different sub-committees of the selectmen and others visited the different schools, ministers were always included on the sub-committees visiting the grammar schools, though not on those visiting exclusively the writing schools.[5] In 1730, when the custom of having one committee visit all the schools was established, the ministers visited all the schools with the rest of the committee.[6] In 1737, six ministers appeared upon the list.[7] All the lists from this time until 1789 include from one to seven ministers.[8]

In 1789 new regulations for the reform of the "System of public Education in Boston" were passed. The law of the

[1] Boston, *Rep. Rec. Com.*, viii., 65, 66.
[2] *Ibid.*, viii., 75, 78.
[3] *Ibid.*, viii., 100.
[4] *Ibid.*, viii., 163.
[5] *Ibid.*, xiii., 134, 153.
[6] *Ibid.*, xiii., 202.
[7] *Ibid.*, xii., 187.
[8] *Ibid.*, xii., 212 *et seq.;* xiv., 9 *et seq.;* xvi., 16 *et seq.;* xviii., 24 *et seq.*

General Court had been enacted a few months before. The new regulations were probably the result of the new interest in education created by that law. Among the provisions for the reform of the system was one which provided that a "Committee be annually chosen by ballot to consist of twelve in addition to the Selectmen, whose business it shall be to Visit the Schools once in every Quarter, and as much oftener as they shall Judge proper." [1] This committee was also to determine the hours of school sessions, to declare play days and advise the masters. In the first election of twelve persons to accompany the selectmen, five were ministers.[2] In 1790 this committee, probably in response to chapter 19 of the acts of 1789, was given authority "to exercise all the powers relating to the Schools & School Masters, which the Selectmen or such Committees are authorized by the Laws of this state or the Votes of this Town to exercise, any former Votes of the Town notwithstanding." [3] There were three or four ministers on every subsequent committee through the year 1796, when the printed records of the town meetings cease.[4]

From the above facts it would seem that the ministers of the town of Boston were active factors in the management of the public schools throughout most of the eighteenth century, and possibly before that time, though the evidence for the earlier period is not at all definite.

Just how far the example set by Boston was followed in other towns of the commonwealth, it is impossible to say. Only a part of the towns had established a regular school committee to serve various school purposes from year to year, before the act of 1789. Among these were Dudley, Lunenburg, Fitchburg, Weston, and Grafton. In none of these cases does the record show that the ordained ministers of the town were ever members of the annual school committees. Assuming that the records would have listed the ministers, as was the case in Boston, it would seem evident that no ministers were on the committees. Nor is there any evidence, so far as the town records go, which would lead one to believe that the ministers

[1] Boston, *Rep. Rec. Com.*, xxxi., 209.

[2] *Ibid.*, xxxi., 211.

[3] *Ibid.*, xxxi., 215.

[4] *Ibid.*, xxxi., 215, 218, 219, 245, 246, 280, 281, 320, 351, 387, 388, 420.

would not be listed because the committees were appointed as additional to the ministers, as was the case in Boston. No such system of appointment is noted in the towns mentioned.

In 1743, Dudley town meeting voted "a committee to provide schooling," according to certain regulations that the meeting had laid down.[1] The town appointed a similar school committee practically every year thereafter until 1792, when the town record closes.[2] A comparison of the list of ministers for this same period,[3] with the list of committeemen on the regular or special school committees, shows not a single minister.

In the case of Lunenberg, as early as 1732 a committee of three "to Provide a School and School Master" was appointed.[4] With the exception of a few isolated years, such a committee is maintained until 1763 at least.[5] The ordained ministers of the town were David Stearns [6] and Samuel Payson.[7] The names of neither one nor the other of these appear as members of the various school committees.

Fitchburg, which was set off from the west part of Lunenburg,[8] followed the custom of appointing school committees which had been prevalent in the parent town. In 1764 a school committee of three was appointed, mainly to provide school masters.[9] A school committee was elected at the town meeting every year for the remainder of the century and on into the next.[10] The committees at no time, prior to 1808, included any of the ministers preaching in the churches of Fitchburg.[11]

The town of Weston did not establish its regular annual school committee until 1796.[12] But before that time it had appointed, with more or less frequency, a number of temporary school committees for various school purposes. These committees appeared between the years 1769 and 1795.[13] The

1 Dudley, *Records*, i., 108, 109.

2 *Ibid.*, i., 128 *et seq.*; ii., 13 *et seq.* There are some few years where the records are not continuous, particularly about 1661–1663. But the record is sufficient to indicate that in general there was an annual committee.

3 *Ibid.*, i., 4.

4 Lunenburg, *Records*, p. 77.

5 *Ibid.*, p. 85 *et seq.*

6 *Ibid.*, pp. 77, 199.

7 *Ibid.*, pp. 198, 211.

8 Fitchburg, *Records*, i., 1, 2.

9 *Ibid.*, i., 7.

10 *Ibid.*, i., 21 *et seq.*; ii., 26 *et seq.*; iv., 8 *et seq.*; v., 4 *et seq.*

11 Torrey, *History of the Town of Fitchburg*, 120–124.

12 Weston, *Records*, i., 467.

13 *Ibid.*, i., 138 *et seq.*

ministers during this period were the Rev. Samuel Woodward[1] and the Rev. Samuel Kendall.[2] Neither of these men had their names upon the town committee for school purposes during the period indicated. In 1796, with the appointment of district committees, the name of minister Kendall appears as one of the third committee.[3]

The town of Grafton had an "annual" committee every year, with the exception of two years, from 1744 until the next century. But no minister appeared as a member of such annual committee until the year 1829.[4]

In no one of the above cases of annual committees for the providing of teachers was a minister a member of the annual committee, prior to 1789, so far as a comparison of lists of ministers and lists of school committees will show. This fact is quite the reverse of that found in Boston, where the annual committee was one for visitation and inspection, and not for the providing of teachers.

There were two other instances where committees of inspection are known to have existed prior to the stimulation of the general law of 1789. The two available records, those of the years 1744 and 1770, of one committee, that of Cambridge, show no ministers.[5] The other committee, that of Lancaster, which was provided for in 1788, had as its chairman, by specific statement of the town vote, "the minister of the town for the time being."[6]

So it would seem that the ministers were not members of most of the annual school committees of the towns. They certainly did not appear upon the more widespread of the two main types of annual committees existing prior to 1789, upon the committee for providing teachers. They seem to have been confined largely to the committees on school visitation and inspection. Even there, there are records which show no ministers on the list of school inspectors. Yet the custom of using

[1] Weston, *Records*, i., 153, 350.

[2] *Ibid.*, i., 331, 524.

[3] *Ibid.*, i., 467.

[4] Clifton, *History of Grafton*, pp. 422–426. *Cf.* Names of ministers in chapter v. of same.

[5] Paige, *History of Cambridge*, p. 375.

[6] Marvin, *History of Lancaster*, pp. 349, 350.

the ministers upon the school committee, where it existed, was a precedent of large importance, for it was incorporated by the General Court in the general school law of the commonwealth in the year 1789.

In 1789, chapter 19 of the acts of that year distinctly conferred upon "the minister or ministers of the Gospel" the duty of visiting the schools of the town or district "once in every six months at least," to inquire into the regulation and discipline thereof, and the proficiency of the scholars therein." They were to be accompanied by the selectmen or school committee.[1] The same section of the law gave to the ministers the responsibility of using their "influence and best endeavours, that the youth of their respective towns and districts do regularly attend the schools." [2]

While this law marked an increase of the power of the ministers in matters of school visitation and inspection, and added the responsibility for the compulsory attendance of children at school, there was a change in the minister's power to certificate teachers. The power of certificating the grammar-school master, which had belonged to the minister exclusively since 1701/2, was now curtailed. The minister's certificate as to the academic fitness of both college and secondary school teachers became purely an option, to be accepted in lieu of evidence of "an education at some College or University." Upon the side of moral fitness, the minister's certificate was not at all necessary if the candidate were a resident of the community where the school was to be kept. If the candidate were applying for a school outside of his own town, the certificate of the selectmen or school committee of his own town would do just as well as the minister's signed statement.[3]

In the matter of elementary teachers, the minister was given some power in certification that he had not possessed before. In addition to the previous certificate of fitness required of selectmen prior to this law, and now issuable from either selectmen or school committee, the prospective teacher was compelled to have a certificate "from a learned minister settled therein, if such there be, that he or she is a person of sober life and conversation, and well qualified to keep such school." [4]

[1] Mass., *Perpetual Laws*, ii., 42, 43.

[2] *Ibid.*, ii., 42.

[3] *Ibid.*, ii., 40, 41.

[4] *Ibid.*, ii., 43.

The phrase, "learned minister . . . if such there be," suggests that perhaps this requirement might be avoided if the authorities hiring the teacher chose to regard the minister as not being learned.

On the whole, the act of 1789 must be regarded as a piece of constructive legislation, so far as the minister's position was concerned. In the matter of school visitation, the practice as found in Boston was incorporated for the entire state. The responsibility for school attendance, whether really amounting to anything or not, was at least a theoretical grant of power. The readjustment of the power of certification certainly was a decided change from the previous laws governing the function.

The law, as a whole, represented the highest power that the ministers, as ministers, ever received by explicit statement of the laws of the commonwealth. Towns which had not included the minister as a governing force in school affairs now followed the suggestion of the law.

But the minister as an officer in school affairs was doomed to pass from the statutes. The sharing of his long-maintained right of certification of grammar-school masters with committees, where they might exist, presaged the complete passing of the minister as an *ex-officio* school officer, as it likewise presaged the passing of the selectman from the management of purely educational affairs. The rise of the school committee marked the decline of the minister's power.

In 1822, Boston was organized as a city, and by special act of incorporation was given a special law. In school affairs, this law provided that a school committee of twelve, one elected from each ward, should "jointly with the Mayor and Aldermen, constitute the School Committee for the said city, and have the care and superintendence of the public schools." [1] No mention was made of ministers. Thus the stronghold of ministerial control in education had passed away from the long-established habit.

The final downfall of the ministerial control in school affairs came in 1826, when practically all the powers previously held by the ministers jointly with selectmen and committees were given into the hands of the school committees which were now made compulsory throughout the commonwealth.[2] The law of

[1] *Acts of 1822*, p. 746.

[2] *Acts of 1826*, chap. clxx.

1827 in its reformulation of previous laws left matters fundamentally as they were in the act of 1826, where the ministers were not even mentioned.[1] It repeated an empty power which had been given the ministers along with others in 1789. This was "the duty of the resident Ministers of the Gospel, the Selectmen, and School Committees, in the several towns in this Commonwealth, to exercise their influence, and use their best endeavours, that the youth of their respective towns, and districts, do regularly attend the Schools."[2]

Thus shorn of the power of certification which they had held in some degree for a century and a quarter, and of their power to inspect schools which they had held jointly with others for more than three decades, the ministers as officers were dismissed from the school affairs with the injunction to "exercise their influence, and use their best endeavours" that all children be educated. Henceforth the minister as such is no longer a school official. Whatever force he remains in school affairs he continues to be because, as a man and citizen, he has enjoyed the confidence of his fellow men, whose suffrage has raised him to the care of their public schools.

CHAPTER V

THE EARLY SCHOOL COMMITTEES, 1639–1725

The shifting of educational supervision from town meeting to selectmen and ministers, and then to the school committees, was a perfectly natural procedure. It is a common trait of human nature to meet its new or more complex situations with its established means. When these have failed even in a slight degree the evolution of new means commences. In the two centuries of American colonial life, educational control and supervision became more and more complex. New problems of school management presented themselves. The effort to meet the educational situation through town meeting, selectmen, and ministers was the utilization of established means, each of which in time proved inadequate for the purpose. The use of special committees to meet some situation of unusual importance or one requiring detailed attention represented the first

[1] *Acts of 1827*, chap. cxliii.

[2] *Ibid.*, chap. cxliii., sec. 3.

groping for a new means. The standing school committee, elected and maintained with regularity, and having as its whole and special function the management of school affairs, was the first agency specially devised and adjusted to the needs of public education.

Some continuous school committees were provided by a few towns, but they were exceptional rather than characteristic, and seem not to have been any large influence upon the method of school management during the early period. The characteristic method of managing school affairs in this first century is that which manifested itself through the town meeting and the town selectmen. Where the committee method of attending to school affairs was used, the purely temporary committee appointed as occasion demanded was the more frequently used. From them, perhaps, rather than from the few isolated and limited uses of the standing school committee, did the later, regularly elected school committees develop.

THE TEMPORARY COMMITTEES

It was not until after the first quarter of the eighteenth century that the towns really used the school committee with regularity for its school business. But the humble beginnings of the movement lay far back in the preceding century, in the custom of appointing erstwhile committees when the business in hand was of such moment as to warrant the detailing of particular persons to the task. The particular thing to be done might have been of any sort: the laying out of school lands, the locating and erecting of a schoolhouse, the finding of a schoolmaster when schoolmasters were scarce, the investigation of crowded conditions, or the repair of buildings. The committee was created to meet an exigency. Once the exigency had passed, the committee passed out of existence. For such matters as might recur with frequency, there were the town meeting and the standing representatives of the town, the selectmen. Hence there was under the modest demands of the school in the first century of colonial life no large and persistent demand for a continuous school committee specially charged with the business of the public school.

There were not many of these special committees during the

first hundred years. Nor did they follow each other with any considerable regularity. Up to the year 1700, Boston did not have more than a half-dozen of these committees.[1] Cambridge, in the same period, had only two of such committees.[2] Dorchester, where the committee idea had taken root unusually early, shows a larger number than either of the preceding places for a shorter period. But the number of committees appointed was comparatively small even there. From 1639 to 1683, excluding the attempted appointment of a permanent committee in 1645 and the naming of the feoffees of the ministry and school lands, there were only about sixteen of such temporary committees, for the forty-four years.[3] In thirty years, from 1642, when the earliest record relating to schools occurs, to 1672, Dedham appointed about eight committees, excluding its feoffees of the school land; an average of about one in four years.[4] Watertown, in the thirty-one years from 1649 to 1680, listed three committees.[5] These committees merely marked the scattered beginnings of the committee idea, which had as yet scarcely attained form as a distinct movement.

In the discussion of the tendency of the town meeting to delegate power in school affairs, it was noted that the first recorded activities of selectmen in educational matters usually appear after a period wherein the town meetings have cared for the school without delegated assistance.[6] The same tendency may be noted with regard to the selectmen and the school committee in this first hundred years under treatment. Just as the town meeting, with its many town cares and a large membership convening only with a certain frequency, was compelled in time to call in the supplementary service of the board of selected townsmen; so these selectmen, still charged with the town's affairs in general, had to be relieved of school affairs by the appointment of special committees on school affairs. Sometimes as soon as the selectmen began to act in school affairs, the use of some sort of a special committee is noted.

[1] Boston, *Rep. Rec. Com.*, vii., 24, 30, 38, 158, 161, 171.

[2] Cambridge, *Records*. pp. 180, 331.

[3] Boston, *Rep. Rec. Com.*, iv., 39, 94, 96, 97, 116, 136, 159, 182, 200, 210 223, 256, 304.

[4] Dedham, *Records*, i., 105, 108, 182, 192, 193; ii., 46, 48, 72, 194.

[5] Watertown, *Records*, pp. 18, 122.

[6] See Chapter II., p. 7 *et seq.*

In the Boston records the selectmen appeared in school affairs in 1644; the first special committee in 1664.[1] The townsmen of Cambridge dealt with the financial affairs of the school as early as 1655. In 1669, these same officials appointed a committee on the taking down of the schoolhouse.[2] In 1682/3 the Braintree town meeting empowered its selectmen to rent the school lands. In 1699, a special committee was utilized for the same purpose.[3] Springfield, in 1679, asked its selectmen to bargain for a place to keep the school. In 1708, it appointed a joint committee of its selectmen and one person from the west side of the town to procure a schoolmaster for that part of the community.[4] Brookline, when it was still known as Muddy-river, in the year 1697, authorized the chosen men of the town to tax the inhabitants for the repairing of the school and other structures. In 1723 the same community was utilizing three committees of two trustees each to manage the affairs of the schools that had been ordered built.[5] In each of these cases the first grant of power to committees occurred later than the first use of selectmen in school affairs.

In some instances the special school committee was called into requisition for particular purposes about as soon as the selectmen, though the general tendency would seem to have been as suggested. Among the examples of towns following the less frequent tendency are Dorchester, which in its first regulations for its school provided that the matter of the instruction of "maydes" be left to a joint committee of selectmen and elders. The same set of regulations left the matter of collecting the school money to some person to be appointed by the selectmen.[6] In 1648 and 1650, the selectmen of Dedham cared for the construction and paid for the repair of the schoolhouse.[7] In 1644 the town appointed a committee of three to lay out land for the charge of the feoffees, but all three were selectmen.[8] In 1651, the selectmen appointed two committees.[9] While the

[1] Boston, *Rep. Rec. Com.*, ii., 82; vii., 22.
[2] Cambridge, *Records*, pp. 109, 180.
[3] Braintree, *Records*, pp. 21, 42.
[4] Springfield, *Records*, i., 413,; ii., 380
[5] Brookline, *Records*, i., 87, 122.
[6] Boston, *Rep. Rec. Com.*, iv., 39.
[7] Dedham, *Records*, i., 123, 132.
[8] *Ibid.*, i., 108.
[9] *Ibid.*, i., 182.

use of committees and selectmen appeared close together, even here the tendency suggests a movement from town to select men, to committees. Watertown appointed a committee of one in the year 1649, and the selectmen appointed the same man to another commission in the same year.[1] Plymouth's earliest use of selectmen occurred in 1672 and 1674, when the selectmen are part of joint committees on the school lands.[2] Later, Plymouth fell into the general tendency and used its selectmen exclusively to get its schoolmasters for a period of ten years; then, in 1703/4, a special school committee of three, none of them selectmen, assumed the duty.[3] Other committees performed the duty later.[4]

The movement from the use of the selectmen to the use of the school committee in school supervision in the broadest sense is marked, not alone by the priority of the use of selectmen. In the beginning of the school committee movement, which is indicated by the more or less sporadic appearance of the special and temporary committees, there are unmistakable signs of the dominance of the selectmen in the early use of the school committee. These signs are to be noted in two factors: (1) in the appointing source of these early committees; (2) in their constitution or membership.

Of the committees noted in Boston during the seventeenth century, all but one were sub-committees appointed by the selectmen and constituted wholly of their own number. In the year 1664, the first record of a school committee for temporary affairs appeared. In that year the selectmen appointed a sub-committee of one of their fellows to lay out the school land,[5] and another sub-committee of two to enlarge the schoolhouse.[6] In 1667 and 1684, committees were appointed to agree with the teacher as to terms.[7] In 1667, one of the selectmen was authorized to inform the widow of the late schoolmaster, Mr. Woodmancey, that the town wished to use the schoolhouse in which she resided.[8] The exceptional case suggested above was that of a committee, consisting only partly of selectmen, appointed by the town meeting, a type which will be considered

[1] Watertown, *Records*, p. 18.

[2] Plymouth, *Records*, i., 124, 140, 141.

[3] *Ibid.*, i., 224, 270, 289, 319.

[4] *Ibid.*, ii., 1, 2 *et seq.*

[5] Boston, *Rep. Rec. Com.*, vii., 30.

[6] *Ibid.*, vii., 32.

[7] *Ibid.*, vii. 38, 171.

[8] *Ibid.*, vii., 51.

as representative of action in another group of towns than that of which Boston is characteristically a member. In 1682, the town meeting of Boston appointed a committee to consider the matter of providing "Free Schooles." It was composed of the town selectmen and the members of a committee on alms and poorhouse.[1]

Cambridge had but two committees during the seventeenth century, so far as the records show. Both of these were appointed by the selectmen, and contained some of their own number as members. In 1669, a committee of two was named for the purpose of agreeing with some suitable person or persons for the tearing down and the rebuilding of the town schoolhouse.[2] In the year 1700, a committee of the same number was delegated to see to the rebuilding of a schoolhouse.[3]

Dedham presented a few scattered school committees during this first century. In the earliest period, when the town meeting was still attending to all its school affairs, the town appointed a committee of three, all selectmen, to lay out certain lands to be placed in the hands of feoffees for the use of the school. This was in 1644, and was the earliest record of school business for that particular town.[4] But the details of school management, following the general trend from town meeting to selectmen, went largely into the hands of the selectmen. The committees appointed thereafter were, with one possible exception, appointed by the selectmen, not the town. This paralleled the method in Boston and Cambridge. In 1651, two sub-committees of selectmen were appointed to contract with workmen for different parts of a school structure.[5] In 1661/2 and 1662, committees of two selectmen each were named to procure and treat with teachers.[6] In 1663 and in 1670, two selectmen were deputed to repair the schoolhouse.[7] It will be noticed that in each case where the selectmen appoint, as in Boston, the committee consisted entirely of selectmen.

Watertown gives further corroboration of the existence of selectmen's committees. From 1649 to 1680 there is a record

[1] Boston, *Rep. Rec. Com.*, vii., 158.
[2] Cambridge, *Records*, pp. 175, 180.
[3] *Ibid.*, pp. 328, 331.
[4] Dedham, *Records*, i., 108.
[5] *Ibid.*, i., 182. [6] *Ibid.*, i., 46, 48. [7] *Ibid.*, i., 72, 194.

of two committees of one, and another of two members, all selectmen. In one case, the earliest school record of the town, the town appointed one "to procuere the Schoole house Built."[1] The same selectman, in the same year of 1649, was appointed by his fellows to issue a call to a schoolmaster in behalf of the town.[2] In 1674, a committee of two selectmen was appointed by the town selectmen to "treat woith the scholmaster."[3]

The tendency of the selectmen to delegate to committees of their own appointment, usually of their own number, the power that the town meeting had delegated to them is in a sense a foreshadowing of the time when the town would appoint its own committees on school affairs directly. The appointment of committees by the selectmen was a recognition of the fact that the selectmen as a whole, like the town as a whole, did not find it easy or efficient to treat special school matters along with the rest of the town's business.

This predominance of selectmen's committees, it will be noted, is associated with a comparatively early portion of the period prior to the second quarter of the eighteenth century, the time when the regularly elected committees began to appear. When the town records of the later portion of this period are studied in communities where the erstwhile school committee occurred, a different set of facts is found. Committees appointed by the town meeting rather than by the selectmen are noted. While selectmen are still represented upon most of these committees, either as part of joint-committees of selectmen and others or as individuals associated with other freemen, the committees, as committees, are very seldom exclusively made up of selectmen of the town.

Braintree was one of the later towns that appointed its school committees in town meeting. In 1694, a committee of three was appointed "to lett & sett all" the school lands.[4] In 1697 and 1699, committees on the erection of schoolhouses were named.[5] In 1699 and 1700 matters pertaining to the schoolmaster were given over to committees.[6] In 1715 and 1716, committees on wood from the school land and the erection of a grammar school, respectively, were appointed.[7] Selectmen were

[1] Watertown, *Records*, p. 18.

[2] *Ibid.*, p. 18. [3] *Ibid.*, pp. 121, 122. [4] Braintree, *Records*, p. 42.

[5] *Ibid.*, pp. 36, 40. [6] *Ibid.*, pp. 41, 46. [7] *Ibid.*, pp. 87, 88.

members of some of these committees. In other cases they were not.

Plymouth, from 1672 to 1725, appointed a considerable number of school committees through its town meeting. These committees were quite as varied in purpose as those that have been mentioned in connection with other towns. The care of the school land, the collecting of school moneys, the erection of schoolhouses, and more frequently the procuring of the schoolmaster were among the purposes served by these temporary boards of freemen. Frequently the committee consisted of selectmen and other freemen. Frequently the committee was named as one of a certain number, and selectmen were merely included among them.[1]

It must not be supposed, however, that all the towns followed one or the other type of action exclusively. Dorchester, for example, was a community that appointed its school committees just about as frequently through the selectmen as through the town meeting. In fact, Dorchester represents an anomalous condition in school affairs on more than one point.

Dorchester, in its very first town vote concerning schools, proceeded to delegate its power in the decision of certain important matters. In 1639, when it voted support, provided for a method of caring for the school moneys, and denominated its method of electing the teacher, it practically named its first school committee by saying that the selectmen and the elders together should settle the question as to whether the girls should be taught along with the boys.[2] Unlike most other towns it started the use of the committee at once, with the very beginning of its existence. In 1645 it proceeded to regulate its school affairs with an attention to details that was totally uncommon to the time.[3] Perhaps because of this very focusing of attention upon so much detail, it felt the necessity of having a special school authority to care for the same. So it created a board of three wardens or overseers of the school, to hold such office, not for the time being, but for life.

Beginning with 1658, the use of temporary committees appeared in Dorchester, as in the other towns, and continued till

[1] Plymouth, *Records*, i., 124 *et seq.;* ii., 1, 2 *et seq.*

[2] Boston, *Rep. Rec. Com.*, iv., 39.

[3] *Ibid.*, iv., 54–57.

1683, when the printed records close.[1] These committees were of the same nature as those found elsewhere, so far as their purpose was concerned. Their method of appointment varied. Sometimes they were appointed by the selectmen as in 1658/9, 1671, and 1681.[2] Sometimes they were appointed by the town meeting, as in 1658, 1663, 1666, 1669, and 1674.[3] The constitution of these also varied. Sometimes the committee was entirely made up of selectmen; sometimes partly so. In other instances no selectmen appeared upon the committee at all.

The mere fact that the selectmen used the committee idea, even to a slight extent, in the conduct of the school affairs with which they were charged, tended to hasten the end of the period in which the selectmen carried the main responsibility for the detailed management of the schools—a period which was purely transitional between the control of the town meeting and the supervision of the annually elected school committee. That hastening tendency is noted further in the increasing use of the special committee for school purposes; in the growing custom of appointing such committees directly through the town meeting, instead of through the selectmen; and also in the lessening presence of selectmen upon the later school committees.

THE STANDING SCHOOL COMMITTEES

It has been suggested that there was some provision among a few towns for standing committees that dealt with school affairs. These committees were known by various terms, such as overseers, wardens, feoffees, trustees, or school committee. They were usually committees or trustees in charge of school lands and funds. In some cases their responsibility was extended to matters that related to educational supervision—that is, to matters which had to do with the instruction given by the teacher rather than with his support alone. As early types of control these feoffees or committees are quite interesting, inasmuch as they represent one particular variation in a period which was marked by more or less groping after means.

Among the instances that may be noted are the feoffees of

[1] Boston, *Rep. Rec. Com.*, iv., 94 *et seq.*

[2] *Ibid.*, iv., 96, 97, 182, 256.

[3] *Ibid.*, iv., 94, 116, 136, 159, 200.

the school at Dedham. In 1644, "At a meeting the first day of the Eleuenth Month—The sd Inhabitants takeing into Consideration the great necessitie of prouiding some meanes for the Education of the youth . . . did . . . declare their willingness to promote that worke promising to put too their hands to prouide maintenance for a Free Schoole in our said Towne." They then pledged themselves to the sum of twenty pounds a year. "And also did resolue & consent to betrust the sd 20 L p annu: & certaine lands in or Towne formerly set apart for publique vse: into the hand of Feofees to be presently Chosen by themselues to imploy the sd 20 L and the land aforesd to be improued for the vse of the said Schoole: that as the profits shall arise from ye sd land euery man may be proportionably abeted of his some of the sd 20 L aforesaid freely to be giuen to ye vse aforesaid And yt ye said Feofees shall haue power to make a Rate for the nesesary charg of improuing the sd land: they giueing account therof to the Towne or to those whome they shall depute." Then follow the names of the feoffees appointed. They were five in number, two of whom were selectmen at the time of appointment.[1] The term of these feoffees was probably an indefinite one. Evidently there was a vacancy in 1648 as the town record shows that one of the matters "to ppose at Genrall meeting" was "that a feoffee for the schoole be chosen."[2] Their function was, in all probability, limited to the express powers quoted, namely, to a financial management of the school funds and lands. There is nothing in the record to indicate that their control went further. On the contrary, other matters were constantly handled by the selectmen or special committees after the year 1648.[3]

Later, a board of trustees came into existence for the purpose of performing functions similar to those of the earlier feoffees. In 1680, Dr. William Avery, of Boston, formerly of Dedham, offered to contribute sixty pounds for the use of the town Latin school.[4] In 1683, the town records show that trustees were appointed and organized for the care of such fund. The record reads: "Ensi Tho Fuller Sergt Daniel Pond and Sergt

[1] Dedham, *Records*, i., 104, 105, 108.

[2] *Ibid.*, i., 155.

[3] *Ibid.*, i., 132 *et seq.;* ii., 2 *et seq.*

[4] Worthington, *History of Dedham*, p. 36.

Tho Metcalfe are desired and impowered wth the Revd elders and Select men to take care of and to dispose of the money aboue saide as it may be secured and improued for the end mentioned." [1] Little is known about the history of this fund. It remained in the hands of trustees for many years, and then disappeared through neglect or malfeasance. [2]

Less than three months after the appointment of the feoffees "for the Schoole" at Dedham, the town of Dorchester embarked upon a far more ambitious plan for a standing school committee. It provided for a committee of three to be called "wardens or oūerseers," who were to have control, not only of the school lands and funds, but of the internal management of the school as well. Beside receiving and disbursing money, and repairing the schoolhouse, the overseers or committeemen were to nominate the schoolmaster for the town's approbation. The town meeting, in creating the school committee, also laid down six long and detailed rules for the government of the school. "Where p'ticular rules are wanting . . . It shalbe a p'te of the office and dutye of the Wardens to order and dispose of all things that Concerne the schoole, in such sort as in their wisedom and discretion they shall Judge most Conducible for the glory of God, and the trayning vp of the Children of the Towne in religion, learning and Civilitie." [3]

This long act of the town meeting passed upon "the 14th of the 1st moneth 1645," provided for a school authority more like the school committee of to-day in many of its features than any other of which there is record in the early colonial period. Its striking resemblance to our modern school committee is so considerable that Dr. William A. Mowry has been led to state that this committee of wardens or overseers "is believed to be the first provision for a school committee in America. From that time till now, public schools have been under the control and management of school committees or directors, or boards of education—whatever the name may have been." [4]

To regard this committee as the first school committee in

[1] *Dedham Historical Register*, 1890, vol. ii., 7.

[2] Worthington, *History of Dedham*, p. 36.

[3] Boston, *Rep. Rec. Com.*, iv., 54–57.

[4] Mowry, Powers and Duties of School Superintendents, *Educational Review*, ix., 39.

America would necessitate a very restricted definition of what constitutes a school committee, for the feoffees of Dedham came before the wardens of Dorchester. The Dedham feoffees were a school committee, with their powers restricted to the management of the school's funds, to be sure, but none the less a committee designed for a continuous and very important school purpose.

To regard this committee as the first, in the sense that it was the first in a long line of committees, the first precedent, in which other committees found their example, so that we find a succession of committees "from that time till now," would be even a more doubtful statement to make. There is no evidence that these wardens ever performed a single service for the school at Dorchester. If its existence, beyond the drawing up of the plan and the election of the overseers, is doubtful, it is unlikely that its importance could have been such as to influence other towns. In fact, its example seems not to be cited by any colonial towns of Massachusetts which through contiguity would be most likely to be influenced. Indeed, there were, so far as can be determined at present, no committees similar to it during the seventeenth century.

Just what became of this school committee has not been determined. When it ceased to exist, or whether or not it ever operated, cannot be stated. A careful tracing of the names of the three original wardens through the town records reveals no mention of the "wardens or overseers," or, in fact, of any school supervisory power, in the form of special appointees.[1] From 1655 on, the records show that powers given to the wardens were being exercised by the selectmen and others.[2] In 1667 there is a reference to "the feffees of the Schol land."[3] The nature of these "feffees," beyond what is suggested in the phrase, is not known, so their relation to the original school wardens who had control of the school lands, if there was any relation at all, is not known.

The notion of a standing school committee was also existent in Roxbury, but under different conditions. Here the school was a matter of agreement between a certain number of the freemen and landholders of the community, rather than a

[1] Boston, *Rep. Rec. Com.*, iv., 54 *et seq.*

[2] *Ibid.*, iv., 73 *et seq.*

[3] *Ibid*, iv., 143.

strictly town affair. In consequence of the corporate nature of the concern, a standing committee of seven feoffees was placed in charge of the affairs of the school. The provision for this standing committee was made in an agreement of the "last of August, 1645," and reads as follows:

> And for the well ordering thereof they have chosen and elected seven Feoffees who shall have power to putt in or remove the Schoolemaster, to see to the well ordering of the schoole and schoolars, to receive and pay the said twenty pounds per annum to the Schoolemaster, and to dispose of any other gifte or giftes which hereafter may or shall be given for the advancement of learning and education of children. [1]

The donors were to elect these feoffees, and if they failed to attend to this matter, the feoffees themselves were to fill vacancies.

To a large extent the duties of these feoffees were much as those assigned to the wardens of Dorchester. In fact, they had more power. Beside the handling of school lands and moneys, "the well ordering of the schoole and schoolars," they had the "power to putt in or remove the Schoolemaster," [2] a power which the wardens of Dorchester did not have. This entire grant of power to the feoffees was, in 1670, confirmed by the General Court in answer to a petition of the feoffees, written because of certain "interruption and opposition." [3]

The powers were not only granted and confirmed, but they were likewise exercised by the feoffees, continuously through the Colonial period. In 1789 the school and its management were re-organized by an act of the General Court.[4] In 1839, by a joint arrangement of the town school committee and the feoffees (now called trustees) of the school, the school itself practically became part of the town school system.[5]

It is more probable that the school feoffees at Roxbury were far more likely to be influential as an example than those of Dorchester, who are known to us merely through a single vote of the town. It is to be remembered in connection with Roxbury, however, that its school was not as strictly a town school

[1] Ellis, *History of Roxbury Town*, p. 135. Dillaway, *Free Schoole of 1645 in Roxburie*, pp. 7–9.

[2] Dillaway, *Free Schoole of 1645 in Roxburie*, p. 8.

[3] *Ibid.*, pp. 15–22.

[4] *Ibid.*, pp. 69, 186 *et seq.*

[5] *Ibid.*, p. 87.

in our modern sense as were those at Dedham and Dorchester.[1] But in the Colonial period, when the public school idea was not what it is to-day, it is somewhat doubtful whether the distinction was felt to the extent of making the Roxbury example much less effective than it would have been had the donors been the whole town instead of "well nigh the whole town in those days."[2] Certainly the matter was confused in the minds of the town people in the decade prior to 1670, for though the General Court required towns to provide teachers of reading and writing, the inhabitants depended upon the "Free Schoole," and would neither contribute to its support nor propose any other plan, even though the feoffees could not receive all the children.[3] In 1666, the donors invited the whole town to join in the work as "most tending to peace and love,"[4] but nothing seems to have been done to settle the controversy until the General Court acted in 1670, when the status of the school as an independent concern of semi-public nature was fixed.[5]

The town of Ipswich, in 1650, co-operated with certain donors in the establishment of a town school, and joint feoffees were appointed for the control of the funds, and perhaps for other matters, though the evidence is not direct. The number of these feoffees was nine for the most part of the time. They were appointed at first by both donors and town. After 1661, vacancies seem to have been filled by the remaining trustees without any interference of the town.[6] In 1720, a difficulty arose between the feoffees and the town. The town contended that, "as respected the School farm and other lands granted by the town, no power was given by the town to their trustees to appoint successors in that trust for receiving and applying the rents, or of ordaining and directing the affairs of the school." The town, through its selectmen, then assumed control of the school and its property, electing a teacher for the ensuing year. The feoffees entered their protest and retired. For twenty-nine years the feoffees were inactive. In 1749, the sole surviving feoffee appointed his fellows and resumed control.[7] In 1755/6,

[1] *Cf.*, Brown, *Making of our Middle Schools*, p. 51.

[2] Dillaway, *op. cit.*, p. 15.

[3] *Ibid.*, p. 29. [4] *Ibid.*, p. 28. [5] *Ibid.*, pp. 15–22.

[6] Hammatt, Address on Anniversary of the Grammar School in Ipswich, *Ipswich Antiquarian Papers*, i., Nos. 2, 3, 4. [7] *Ibid.*, i., No. 10

an act of the General Court provided for a joint committee of four feoffees and the three senior selectmen of the town, who were given authority, not only over the finances of the school, but were likewise definitely given other powers of a supervisory nature: "to appoint grammar-school masters from year to year," "to inspect said school and schoolmaster," etc.[1] In 1765/6, the law was re-enacted for a period of ten years[2]; in 1787, the act was made perpetual.[3]

Hadley records another example of feoffees or trustees with life term in the management of school funds. The school committee for the care of the Hopkins and other funds which might come to the grammar school, was appointed in 1669. It was a committee of five to act with a Mr. Goodwin, one of the surviving trustees of the Hopkins School Fund. Three of the members were appointed by Mr. Goodwin and two by the town. Its control continued, with a single period of disturbance, until 1816, when the committee became the "Trustees of the Hopkins Academy," under an act of the legislature.

The single period of disturbance needs to be noted. In 1686, the town tried to control the foundation of the school; to "take it into their hands to manage, order, and dispose to the use of a school in this town of Hadley."[4] The school in mind was an English school. The president and council overruled the town and confirmed the grants to the regular trustees for a Latin Grammar school.[5]

Just what influence the existence of these various school feoffees had in moulding the school committee as the special form for managing and supervising the public school will probably never be determined, because of lack of evidence. There were certain facts about these committees which would tend to lessen their influence in setting the pattern for methods of school management which have led to those of to-day.

The management of lands and funds seems to have been the main purpose of these committees. It is the one function that all these early standing committees have in common. It was

[1] Mass., *Prov. Acts & Res.*, iii., 891–893.
[2] *Ibid.*, iv., 806–808.
[3] Hammatt, *op. cit.*, *Ipswich Antiquarian Papers*, i., No. 10.
[4] *Amer. Jour. of Educ.*, xxvii., 147, The Hopkins Foundation.
[5] *Ibid.*, xxvii., 148.

practically the entire purpose of both the standing school boards that were found in Dedham. In the "rules and orders" of the Dorchester school, the very first section concerning duties is devoted to the school "stock," with its "Rents, Issues, and p'fitts." The rules for the school were largely made by the town meeting. Only powers not mentioned in a particular rule could be exercised by the wardens. The teacher had to be approved by the town. The other committees in Roxbury, Ipswich, and Hadley, all came into existence because the gifts of donors to the school, rather than to the town, required a special agency of control, since the town or the selectmen were not properly available. Such management of local school funds in the case of our modern public schools devolves upon the town meeting or selectmen, as representatives of the town.[1] Even the state school fund moneys go into the hands of the town treasurer until disbursed by the school committee.[2] The school committee is a committee which has primarily to do with the actual management of the details of the conduct of the school itself, not with the care of its support. In the histories of the committees which persisted to the time of the establishment of public school committees, there is no record of one becoming a town committee. They remained the trustees of a particular school with its school fund. To be sure, the schools at Roxbury and Ipswich became part of the town system, but the integrity of the feoffees or trustees was kept distinct even then.

The fact that membership upon these committees was practically for life is a characteristic which sharply differentiated this movement from that other tendency which was making toward annually elected town and district committees. The life trustees of these few town schools did not show any tendency to change their term of election even when the other movement was in full swing. The Ipswich committee, to be sure, came to have selectmen as three of its number, but the original feoffees were still elected for life.

There is no evidence of transition upon two important points of difference. But the lack of potent influence on the part of these feoffees may be shown in a less negative manner. The towns through their town meetings, which, as will be shown

[1] Mass., *Rev. Laws Relating to Public Instruction*, 1904, chap., 42, secs. 22, 23, 24.

[2] *Ibid.*, chap. xli., sec. 3.

later, were tending to develop the town and district committees elected at town or district meetings, were actually antagonistic to these "closed corporation" school committees. The feoffees of Roxbury encountered "interruption and opposition" from the inhabitants of the town, who would neither help support the school nor provide another.[1] An appeal had finally to be made to the General Court to settle the matter. This was in 1669.[2] The town of Ipswich actually took the control of the school and lands away from the feoffees for a period of twenty-nine years. This was in 1720.[3] The Hadley custodians of the Hopkins foundation had a similar experience. In 1686 the town tried to take control of the funds for the purpose of diverting the same to its own project for another type of school. Only through the order of the President and Council were the trustees protected.[4]

These standing school committees of the particular town secondary schools, with their self-perpetuating membership and life tenure, represented a different movement than that out of which the town committees of the later eighteenth and early nineteenth century arose. They were the natural administrative accompaniment of the movement toward the establishment of semi-public and endowed secondary schools of the English type. The form of government, like the form of school, was patterned after English models.[5] With that other movement, which ended in the establishment of annually elected town and district committees for the public schools, these standing school committees of particular secondary schools had little in common save the mere committee idea. The temporary committees of the towns and the standing committees of particular schools represented two different movements in educational administration and supervision.

In this first hundred years of colonial life two distinct phases of the committee movement are noted. Upon the one hand, is the use in some few cases of continuous school committees, which tend, if they are not so already, to become self-perpetuating bodies with life tenure for its members. They arose usually

[1] Mass., *Prov. Acts & Res.*, iii., 891–893; iv., 806–808.

[2] Dillaway, *op. cit.*, 15 *et seq.*

[3] Hammatt, *op. cit.*, *Ipswich Antiquarian Papers*, i., No. 10.

[4] *Amer. Jour. of Educ.*, xxvii., 147, 148, The Hopkins Foundation.

[5] Cf Taunton, *Great Schools of England*, p. 186 *et seq.;* p. 212 *et seq.*

(though not always) in connection with the endowment of particular schools through the gifts of lands and moneys by donors. Upon the other hand, are the temporary committees appointed for all sorts of school duties, dependent for their existence and their continuance upon the will of the town meeting, whose agents they were. The distinct outgrowth of school government through the town meeting and the selectmen, they are of great importance, for from them, it will later be seen, developed the American school committee of the nineteenth century.

CHAPTER VI

THE DEVELOPMENT OF THE COMMITTEE FOR PROCURING TEACHERS, 1700–1789

The annual school committees of the nineteenth century had their origin in the practice of appointing committees of the town, to attend to such school matters as were of such importance or of such detail as to require more attention than the town meeting, or its selectmen, with their many town duties, could properly give. As has been seen, these committees served various exigencies. When the town had properly met its difficulty for the time being, with the aid of its special committee, the committee passed out of existence.

Among all the purpose which these special and temporary committees were designed to serve, there were some representing problems or situations, which were more likely to persist and recur than others. Obviously, a committee upon the procuring of a school teacher was more likely to be required again, than a committee upon the building of a schoolhouse; one upon the locating of schools during the period of "moving schools" in the early eighteenth century, than one upon determining the school site during a period of "fixed schools" in the seventeenth century; one upon inspection of the teacher who might change each year, than one upon the sale of school lands.

It was this tendency of certain situations to recur or persist which led to the development of the annual school committee from the practice of appointing temporary committees for special school affairs. Out of all the uses to which the temporary committee had been put, as seen in the preceding chapter, there were two which tended to persist or recur more than any of the others. These were the need of providing teachers for the schools, and the need to inspect the quality of their work. The other committees of all sorts, from a committee on repairs to one on a general reform of the arrangement of schools, were contributory to a greater or less extent in establishing the school committee, but these two needs mentioned—the hiring of the teacher and the inspection of his work—represented the two persisting situations which did most to bring about a regular recurrence in the appointment of school committees.

The school act of the year 1789 was the first recognition given by the General Court to school committees as a general method of attending to school affairs. This law laid the responsibility for certification and visitation of schools jointly upon the ministers and selectmen or school committees. In the sections upon certification, existing school committees are not only recognized as a substitute for the selectmen in the exercise of a joint power, but the kinds of existing committees are definitely mentioned. There are two kinds of committees in the then current practice which are definitely mentioned: (1) the "Committee, who may be authorized to hire such schoolmaster,"[1] and (2) "the committee appointed by such town, district, or plantation to visit their schools."[2] Committees for hiring teachers and committees for inspection of the work of teachers—these are the two types of committees which became annual committees, and were recognized by the State in its first recognition of the school committee as a means of school supervision.

The last three quarters of the eighteenth century is the period of transition wherein these two types of committees were developed. In that time they became prominent above the various committees with other purposes. In that time they gradually recurred with greater frequency until they were continually elected annually. In that time they tended, the committee of visitation where the town was still the main unit, and the committee on teachers where the district was most important, to gather other duties to themselves, until, in 1827, the State definitely formulated the town school committee and the district prudential committee, and gave to each certain specific powers[3]

[1] Mass., *Perpetual Laws*, chap. xix., sec. 6.

[2] *Ibid.*, chap. xix., sec. 10.

[3] *Acts of 1827*, chap. cxliii.

It will be necessary to trace the development of these two important types of committees, which came into existence because of two important needs. These two needs did not play the same part in every community. A progressive town such as Boston, the centre of culture and industry, was less likely to find teachers difficult to obtain. The university which supplied the grammar-school masters was almost within its boundaries. In such a community teachers were not only likely to be available, but it likewise would be probable that higher educational standards would obtain in such a town. Such would seem to have been the case as it was the committee of inspection, not the committee for the procuring of teachers, which was found in the Boston of the eighteenth century.

Upon the other hand, a town such as Lunenburg, or Fitchburg, which was detached from it, remote from the college at Cambridge and other centers of educational activity, with a sparse population spread over many districts, each district demanding a schoolmaster of its own, was more likely to feel the need of schoolmasters, and of such agency as might insure their being obtained. Such would seem to have been the case as it was the committee on the procuring of teachers, not the committee of inspection, which was found in Lunenburg and Fitchburg.

The development of each of these two movements may, perhaps, be best suggested by an account of the development of each kind of committee under the typical conditions which brought them forth; the committee on teachers as developed in Lunenburg and Fitchburg taken as one movement,[1] and the committee on inspection of schools as developed in the town of Boston. Since the need of teachers was an influence felt considerably prior to the idea of school inspection, its beginnings may be traced first.

The records of school activity in Lunenburg commence with the year 1732. A school committee appeared in this very year. It was a committee of five "to Provide a School and School Master for to teach Children and youth to Read and write & if the Comtte See Good to hire a Gramer School master, they Shall have ye Liberty."[2] The master hired evidently taught

[1] Fitchburg was a part of Lunenburg until the year 1764, when it was set off as a town by itself. Fitchburg, *Records*, i., 1, 2.

[2] Lunenburg, *Records*, p. 77.

his allotted months and left, for the need of a schoolmaster arose again the following year, when the town voted to hire a schoolmaster for three months.[1] Three months' labor could scarcely keep a master in a place the year round, unless the master was a resident of the town. But another master was at hand, and the town meeting elected him without the help of selectmen or special committee.[2] The three months ended again, and the time for schooling again arriving, the same demand for a teacher was felt, and this time a special committee for that purpose was again the resort. Three men were appointed to provide a master, to agree with him, and to provide three places in which he was to keep the school.[3] Then for two years the selectmen attended to school matters, providing places and "School Dames."[4] In 1737, when a "School Master" was needed, there was a committee of three appointed to "be a Committee to hire a School Master and to provide places for ye School to be keept in this present year,"[5] thus reviving the committee again. A month later, in July of 1737, another committee for the same purpose was chosen.[6] Such committees were annually elected through the year 1740.[7] Then for two years the selectmen attended to the matter.[8] The following year, 1743, the committee of three to provide a schoolmaster and places for a school again appeared among the records of the same meeting at which the other town officers were elected.[9] The following two years the committee was still elected with the other town officers.[10] With this reappearance of the school committee on teachers and places for the school in the year 1743, the town school committee was elected regularly each year until the town of Fitchburg was detached from Lunenburg in 1764.[11]

Thus the regularly elected annual school committee of the town of Lunenburg had come into existence in response to the need for some agency to insure a supply of teachers, and to procure places for the keeping of the traveling school. First, there came a committee for this purpose just as any other committee

[1] Lunenburg, *Records*, p. 83.
[2] *Ibid.*, p. 83.
[3] *Ibid.*, p. 85.
[4] *Ibid.*, pp. 89, 94, 95.
[5] *Ibid.*, p. 97.
[6] *Ibid.*, p. 97.
[7] *Ibid.*, pp. 102, 105, 108. In 1739, the committee consisted of one instead of three.
[8] *Ibid.*, pp. 112, 115.
[9] *Ibid.*, p. 118.
[10] *Ibid.*, pp. 122, 125.
[11] *Ibid.*, pp. 118, 122, 125, 129, 131–133, 137 *et seq.*

would be appointed, as a sort of temporary delegation of power. A lapse of one year, then the committee is used again. Another lapse of two years and another restoration; this time five committees were appointed in four successive years. Another dropping of the committee, and, finally, the committee came to be a regular matter elected each year, frequently with the rest of the town officers. In the period from 1732 to 1763, two periods are distinctly marked: the period of transition from occasional to annual committees, and the period of the established annual committee. In the transition period of the first eleven years, there were seven committees, two of which were appointed in one year. In the period of the established annual committee, there were twenty-one annually elected committees in twenty-one years.

The size and membership of these committees varied somewhat, but there was considerable uniformity on the whole. In size the trend was from the committee of three toward the committee of five. The first committee in 1732 was one of five.[1] All the committees of the transition period and of the period of the established annual committees through the year 1745 were committees of three, save in one instance.[2] In 1739, there was, apparently, but one on the committee.[3] From 1746 through the year 1763, the number named upon the committees was five, save in the year 1752, when it was temporarily reduced to three.[4]

On all the committees in the period which has been spoken of as transitional—that is, the period during which school committee and selectmen alternated more or less in the providing of schools—there was always one member who at the same time was a selectman of the town.[5] None of the first three committees after 1743, when the annual committees became established, had selectmen as members.[6] The tendency seemed to be, not only in a direction away from the use of the selectmen as an organized body, but also away from the use of selectmen as members of the school committees, now there they had come to be an established body for school affairs.

When the west part of Lunenburg continued its separate

[1] Lunenburg, *Records*, p. 77.
[2] *Ibid.*, p. 83 *et seq.*
[3] *Ibid.*, p. 105.
[4] *Ibid.*, p. 129 *et seq.*
[5] *Ibid.*, p. 77 *et seq.*
[6] *Ibid.*, pp. 117, 118, 121, 122, 124, 125.

existence as the town of Fitchburg, it immediately proceeded to manage its schools after the manner its inhabitants had known while under the domain of the town of Lunenburg. While the town of Lunenburg had of late been using a committee of five, the first school committee of Fitchburg, the one chosen in 1764, was a committee of three. Its functions were evidently the same as those committees that have been noted in Lunenburg, namely, to hire the schoolmaster and provide the places for schooling.[1]

Every year after 1764, the town of Fitchburg elected and maintained a school committee out of its own initiative, as a local custom until, in 1826, the law of the commonwealth, requiring every town to maintain such a committee, made the continued choice of such a committee obligatory.[2] During that period the tendency was for the size of the committee to increase and for its functions to expand.

From 1764 until 1773, the committee was a committee of three.[3] In 1773, there was a report on "quartring the Scols," which was rejected by the town.[4] It is probable that some new method of districting was agreed upon before the next choice of a school committee, as the committee elected in 1774 was made one of five members.[5] It continued of this size through the year 1779.[6] In 1780, the committee was made one of six. It is probable that this committee on schools had, from a very early date, partaken of the nature of a committee representative of the various districts of the town. In this year the district arrangement seems to have been very definite in the organization of the committee, for it was "voted that Each Committee man Draw his part of the Towns money according to their valuation." [7] With the exception of one year,[8] the committee remained one of six members through the year 1789.[9] In 1790, the town was again redistricted into seven parts and

[1] Fitchburg, *Records*, i., 7.

[2] *Ibid.*, i., 7 *et seq.;* ii., 20 *et seq.;* iv., 8 *et seq.;* v., 4 *et seq.*

[3] *Ibid.*, i., 7, 21, 27, 43, 55, 62, 64, 78, 83, 90, 91, 101.

[4] *Ibid.*, i., 91.

[5] *Ibid.*, i., 101.

[6] *Ibid.*, i., 117, 133, 160, 183, 201.

[7] *Ibid.*, i., 217, 218.

[8] *Ibid.*, i., 325. The committee in 1786 was one of five.

[9] *Ibid.*, i., 217, 236, 257, 270, 288, 306, 356, 381; ii., 20.

seven committeemen were chosen, under a vote of the town which expressly stated "that there shall be a Committee man Choose to each Destrict yearly they to be under the Directions of the Destrict they belong." [1] This committee, representing the districts as it did, grew as the number of districts increased, through the next two or three decades. In 1798, there were ten members upon the committee [2]; in 1799, there were eleven "to be School Committeemen in the Several destricts to which they belong." [3] This number was increased to twelve in 1812,[4] which was still the number upon the committee for school districts in 1827,[5] when the district prudential committee was made obligatory by law of the state.[6]

The committee appointed upon the hiring of teachers for the various districts tended not only to expand as the number of districts it served increased, but it likewise tended to grow in extent of functions exercised. In 1764, when Fitchburg set up its own school committee, it was for the purpose of providing schooling or schoolmasters, as was the case with the committees previously appointed, when Fitchburg was still a part of the old town of Lunenburg.[7] In 1766, the committee received additional discretionary power in the disbursing of money. When the town voted its eight pounds of school money, it expressly stated that after two thirds of the money had been laid out for schooling in the middle of the town, the rest of the money was "to be Laid out by the Commity as they Shall think proper on the out sides off the Town." [8] In 1776, actual regulative and supervisory authority was given to the school committee when the town "Voted to impower the Schools Committee to Give orders to such Master or Masters as they shall imploy in said Service." [9] It gave the power of supervision, at least, though it did not specifically impose inspection and examination of schools as the basis for such regulation as the later law of the commonwealth did.[10]

The development of the school committee out of the need of supplying teachers, as found in Lunenburg and Fitchburg, is

[1] Fitchburg, *Records* ii., 42, 45.
[2] *Ibid.*, iv., 130.
[3] *Ibid.*, iv., 161.
[4] *Ibid.*, v., 45.
[5] *Ibid.*, v., 304.
[6] *Acts of 1827*, chap. cxliii., sec. 6.
[7] Fitchburg, *Records*, i, 7.
[8] *Ibid.*, i., 27.
[9] *Ibid.*, i., 133.
[10] *The Acts of 1789, 1826, and 1827.*

quite representative. Other towns in which this type of committee became a factor parallel the stages noticed there, with some slight variations due to local causes for the most part. In some cases the committees start much later or develop much more slowly, but they run about the same course, if the committee were developed at all before the laws of the General Court became an influencing element. A few of these may be noticed, briefly, by wav of corroboration.

When the warrant for the regular town meeting for March, 1737, was issued in the town of Dudley, there was included a clause which read as follows: "2) to hire schoolling for our children a reading school for summer and a writing school for winter and likewise to chuse a committee to provide for schooling." [1] Nothing seems to have been done about it. The interesting fact here is that, like Lunenburg and Fitchburg, the idea of a committee on the provision of schooling was associated from the start as the method of setting up a school. In the case of the earlier communities, the town meeting as a whole, or the selectmen, would have been mentioned to the neglect of the school committee. There was another mention of the necessity of providing schooling two years later, in the warrant for the town meeting and something was done. The town provided a schoolhouse, levied a rate, and arranged to let the east and west ends of the town draw their own money, thus practically establishing the district system.[2]

The following year a committee of three, one to represent each district, was appointed "a Commitey to devide the Town into three parts as thay shall subcribe and each part is to pay whear they subcribe." [3] Thus the first committee was distinctly drawn on district lines, as was not true to such an extent of the earliest Lunenburg and Fitchburg committees. From now on, the basis for the appointment of committees is the number of districts in the town. It will be noticed that this committee does not seem to have been instructed to hire the teacher. But once the question of support was no longer in the stage of establishment, the committees were distinctly for that one purpose.

With the year 1743, the town appointed its first committee

[1] Dudley, *Records*, i., 73.

[2] *Ibid.*, i., 73, 76.

[3] *Ibid.*, i., 91.

"to provid schooling." [1] Such a committee became a regular annual committee from that time on until 1761, when some distrust of the school committee regarding financial matters having arisen, the town ceased to appoint a committee, and gave the selectmen the control of school affairs, at the same time naming three citizens "to recond with Captt Newell town treasurer and with the school committees in the years 1759 and 1760 and to bring in there account at our next may meeting." [2] There was evidently some reason for such suspicion, as the accounts of several district committeemen were rejected later.[3]

The result of this discontinuance of the committee meant that the committee idea had to struggle for establishment again. Not until 1764 did the committee reappear.[4] It is shown on the town record about every other year for a while.[5] Beginning with the year 1770, the committee was an annual committee again and continued as such.[6]

The number of the committee was determined by the number of districts in the town from the beginning. It was a committee of three from 1743 to 1760, when it became one of five.[7] In 1762, the town was redistricted into six parts, and the first committee thereafter, in 1764, was made up of the same number.[8] From 1772 on, the number on the committee was seven.[9]

This committee, which through the earlier period was referred to as "a committee to provide for schooling for the present year," later, with the year 1770, came to be called the "School Committee for the Insuing year." [10] The very permanence and regularity of the school committee is implied in that change of terminology. Later, the dual nature of the school committee as a town and a district affair came to be expressed, for the terms "School Committee" and "School Committees" were used interchangeably for the seven men appointed.[11]

The town of Grafton maintained an annual school committee from the year 1744 on into the next century, with the exception of two individual years.[12] In 1764, no committee was chosen.

[1] Dudley, *Records*, i., 108, 109.
[2] *Ibid.*, ii., 60, 64.
[3] *Ibid.*, ii., 70.
[4] *Ibid.*, ii., 84.
[5] *Ibid.*, ii., 98, 113.
[6] *Ibid.*, ii., 123, 133, 137, 144, 145, 150 *et seq.*
[7] *Ibid.*, i., 108 *et seq.*; ii., 13 *et seq.*; 54.
[8] *Ibid.*, ii., 66, 84.
[9] *Ibid.*, ii., 137 *et seq.*
[10] *Ibid.*, ii., 123.
[11] *Ibid.*, ii., 216, 240.
[12] Clifton, *History of Grafton*, pp. 422–426.

The same was true in 1771, when the selectmen acted as a school committee.[1] They are the only two exceptions in the long period of time.

There was, prior to 1744, the same transition period from selectmen and temporary committee to annual committee that has been noted in Lunenburg, Fitchburg, and Dudley. The use of the school committee seems to date from about the time of the introduction of the district system. Before 1737 the school was kept in one place only.[2] In 1736, a temporary committee of three was chosen to "procure" a schoolmaster. In the very same year another such committee was called into requisition for a master for the ensuing year.[3] In 1737, the school committee was made up of five selectmen.[4] In 1738, and 1739, there were school committees made up of freemen, one member of the first committee being at the same time a selectman. Then the selectmen attended to schools in 1740; a school committee of five in 1741; the selectmen again in 1742 and 1743. In 1744, as has been stated, the long-continued use of the annual committee began.[5]

Through the year 1756, selectmen were intermittently members of the school committee. After that time the same person seemed not to have held the two offices, a tendency similar to that noted in other towns, and indicating the trend away from the control of the selectmen.[6]

The number upon the committee in this particular town seems to have been five most of the time from 1737 until 1785.[7] In that year it changes to seven; in the following year to eight; in the next year to nine. It remains at nine until 1797, when it changes to ten members.[8]

The need for some agency that would insure teachers for the school was a force that tended to bring about the annual election of committees for this purpose, particularly in those remoter quarters as yet sparsely settled, where the town was divided into many districts, so that each family might have a school within convenient distance of the home. The increased demand for teachers due to the district system, and the remoteness of these towns from centers of culture, contributed to

[1] Clifton, *History of Grafton*, p. 423
[2] *Ibid.*, p. 257.
[3] *Ibid.*, p. 259.
[4] *Ibid.*, pp. 412, 422.
[5] *Ibid.*, p. 422.
[6] *Ibid.*, pp. 422, 423.
[7] *Ibid.*, pp. 422–424.
[8] *Ibid.*, p. 424.

increase their need above that of such communities as Boston, Brookline, and Braintree, which were not very remote from the college at Cambridge.

The ultimate outcome of this persisting need for a teacher each year was the development of the plan of having a committee elected each year for the purpose of supplying teachers. They tended to reflect the district system in their organization, each individual member of such annual committee tending to be primarily responsible for duties in his own district, rather than for the entire town. While the committee usually found its origin in the need of teachers, such committees, as time passed, tended to add by slow degrees certain other powers, such as responsibility for financial management of funds for disbursement, the finding of suitable places for the schools, and, finally, general management of the school itself.

CHAPTER VII

THE DEVELOPMENT OF THE COMMITTEE FOR SCHOOL INSPECTION, 1700–1789

If Fitchburg (with Lunenburg) represented the development of the school committee for the general care and superintendence of its public schools, through the broadening of the powers of a committee which originated in the need to provide teachers, the town of Boston represented the evolution of the school committee for general educational purposes out of an annual committee appointed for the inspection of instruction in the schools.

The committee for school inspection represented a far more advanced idea than the committee for the procuring of teachers, and its period of development through the local will of the towns is somewhat later. General regulation of the schools there always was to a certain degree. The town meeting and the selectmen indulged in a certain regulation of the schools, as apart from the questions of support and hiring a teacher, the two fundamental matters in the very beginning. The term of the school, the subjects to be taught, the length of the daily session, the providing of fuel, the fixing of the school rate upon the children,—these were all, in a way, matters of regulation.

But they had little to do with the actual relations of teacher and pupils under the conditions of instruction and discipline. Such regulation was done with knowledge out of hand. It was not based upon anything equivalent to visitation of schools.

There had been some regulation of the teacher and his work in a rather crude but perhaps efficient way. Teachers had been dismissed by the authority caring for the schools. In 1666, Mr. Jones was "forbideng to keep schoole any longer" by the Boston authorities.[1] In 1678, the selectmen of Watertown discontinue the services of two teachers and hire another.[2] Salem, in the same century, in 1699, goes further and instructs its selectmen thus: "You shall give ye Gramer school master such instructions and directions, as you shall think needfull for regulation of ye schoole." [3] But that such regulation or dismissal was founded upon the preliminary service of visitation and inspection, is not at all indicated by the records. The function of visitation, so far as the available evidence goes, was not recognized distinctly as such until the following century. Boston seems to be the first of the towns to give it this recognition, and the movement toward committees of visitation and inspection may be best studied by tracing the growth of the idea in the town of Boston.

The earliest Boston committees on school affairs, appointed by the selectmen for the most part, have already been discussed. After that vote of 1689, by which the town restored "the former Custome & practice in managing the affaires of the free schools," [4] there were no more school committees utilized until 1709, when a most important committee of seven was appointed "to consider of the affaires relateing to the Gram̄er Free School of this Town, and to make report thereof at the Town meeting in March next." [5]

This committee, after conference with the ministers, submitted a report which is exceedingly important, because it established a school visitation committee which seems to have been the model for such committees for the following century. In March, 1709/10, the town accepted the report, and proceeded to "Nominate and Appoint a Certain Number of Gentlemen, of

[1] Boston, *Rep. Rec. Com.*, vii., 32, 33.

[2] Watertown, *Records*, p. 137.

[3] Felt, *Annals of Salem*, i. 438, 439.

[4] Boston, *Rep. Rec. Com.*, vii., 197.

[5] *Ibid.*, viii., 63.

Liberal Education, Together with Some of ye Revd Ministers of the Town to be Inspectors of the Sd Schoole under that name Title or denomination." They were "To Visit ye School from time to time, when and as Oft, as they shall thinck fit to Enform themselves of the methodes used in teaching of ye Schollars and to Inquire of their Proficiency, and be present at the performance of Some of their Exercises, the Master being before Notified of their Comeing, And with him to consult and Advise of further Methods for ye Advancement of Learning and the Good Government of the Schoole."[1]

The result of the town's acceptance of this report was the appointment of a committee of five persons beside the ministers. In the following March, a year later, five members to act with the ministers were again chosen.[2] There is no further record of the election of such a committee after this time. Two short years is the period of its operation so far as can be learned. And little is known as to the actual activity of the committee during even this short period.

This committee was the first committee on school inspection in the town of Boston of which we have any definite, official mention. In fact, it seems to be the earliest committee given the definite duty of visitation of which there is any record in the commonwealth of Massachusetts. The report of the committee which recommended the appointment of such inspectors, to be sure, prefaced their recommendation with words which implied some precedent. This introductory clause is as follows: "We further propose and recommend, as of Great Service and Advantage for the promoting of Diligence and good literature, That the Town Agreeably to the Usage in England, and (as we understand) in Some time past practiced here do Appoint a Certain Number of Gentlemen," etc.[3] But the very vagueness of tone in the reference seems to imply, likewise, that the gentlemen of the committee were not at all sure.

This committee did not have supervisory power over the teacher and his work, in the modern sense of the word "supervision." The inspection of schools, a power which this committee did exercise, led to that in a far later period. Such inspection as this committee was intended to exercise might have been a basis for the town's opinion of the work of the school,

[1] Boston, *Rep. Rec. Com.*, viii., 65. [2] *Ibid.*, viii., 75. [3] *Ibid.*, viii., 65.

but it was not yet the preliminary to actual directive control of the teacher and his work on the part of the committee. The committee's relations to the teacher were purely advisory; the committee might merely "consult and Advise of further Methods for ye Advancment of Learning and the Good Government of the Schoole." [1]

It will be noted that this was not a committee upon the visitation of all the town schools, but merely of the "Gram̄er Free School." And the power of this committee for this single school was, in the vote of establishment, restricted to visitation of the school and advisory consultation with the master. But the powers of the committee tended to expand from the start. At the same meeting at which the inspectors were appointed, they were given the additional power of agreeing with the old and the new ushers. They were even allowed to hire the latter.[2] Thus, with the very beginning of the school inspection committee in Boston, there is a tendency to confer upon such body that power which was the source of those annual committees which have been noted in other towns, namely, the hiring of teachers.

The last mention of this committee of ministers and five inspectors is noted in connection with a most interesting memorial presented to the town by the selectmen, who asked that the same be referred "to the Inspectors of the School, and Ministers of the Town." The opening paragraph of the memorial is as follows:

> Whereas according to the Information of Some of the Learned, who have made Observation of the easie & pleasant Rules and Methodes used in Some Schools in Europe, where Schollars p'haps within the compass of one year, have attained to a Competent Proficiency So as to be able to read, and discourse in Lattin and of themselves capable to make Considerable progress Therein: And that according to the methodes used here Very many hundreds of boyes in this Town, who by their parents were never designed for a more Liberal Education have Spent two, three, four years or more of their more Early dayes at the Lattin School, which hath proved of very Little, or no benefit as to their after Accomplishmt.[3]

There is no mention that the committee did anything in the matter, for the committee itself disappears from the record with the vote that refers this memorial to them.

[1] Boston, *Rep. Rec. Com.*, viii., 65. [2] *Ibid.*, viii., 66. [3] *Ibid.*, viii., 78.

The membership of this committee was, as the vote states, one of "five persons" in addition to the ministers of the town. The same five persons were named in the two succeeding years of the recorded existence of the committee.[1] No selectmen were included among these five "Gentlemen, of Liberal Education,"[2] though the selectmen had had much to do in the management of all the schools hitherto, and continued to care, to a large extent, for the affairs of the writing schools after the committee for the "Grām̄er Free School" was created.[3]

Shortly after the time of this Latin school committee, in March of 1712/3, it was "Voted That a Cōmittee Shall be raised to Inspect the Free writing Schools which are Supported at the Townes Charge, And Also to Treat wth Mesues Hutchinsons relating to what they have proposed towards ye Encouragemt of a writing School at the North, and to make report to ye Town at their meeting of what they Shall think proper relating thereto."[4] Whether or not this committee was intended to be a committee for inspecting the writing schools as the previous committee on the Latin school was, cannot be definitely determined. The committee may have been intended for this purpose, but it seems not to have served it. Seemingly the committee devoted itself to fostering one new school, and more particularly to the proper accommodating of that school.[5] The following March, the committee reported and the report was referred to as "relating to a writeing School at the North." The report was at this time referred back to the original committee, which was to act with the selectmen in the further consideration of the same.[6] In May of 1714, the whole business of the committee ended in instructions to the selectmen to purchase a lot for a school building, rather than in any purely educational matter, since it was "Pursuant to a Return of the Committee" that the town "Voted. That it be left with the Selectmen to purchase a peice of Land Sutable to Sett a School House on there."[7]

The first committee of inspection referred only to the Latin school, and, so far as the records show, was elected only two

[1] *Cf.* Boston, *Rep. Rec. Com.*, viii., 65, 66, 75.
[2] *Cf. ibid.*, viii., 64–66.
[3] *Ibid.*, viii., 90, 93, 94, 101 *et seq.*
[4] *Ibid.*, viii., 94.
[5] *Ibid.*, viii., 139.
[6] *Ibid.*, viii., 101.
[7] *Ibid.*, viii., 103.

successive years. Then there is a gap of two years, 1712 and 1713, in which no inspectors of the grammar school were appointed, so far as can be determined by the examination of the records.

In March of 1713/4 the committee of inspection was revived, but with some very important changes from the previous organization of the committee in 1710 and 1711. In fact, it will be noticed that with each revival of the committee of inspection after a period of non-existence, important changes were made. The vote of re-establishment read:

"Voted. That ye Sel:men together with the Reverend Ministers of this Town be desired to be the Inspectors of the Free Grammar Schools for the year ensuing." [1] There are two distinct changes to be noted in the organization of these inspectors, as opposed to those holding office in 1710 and 1711. In the first place, the committee was no longer a committee of a particular school, but of a grade of schools. In November, 1711, the town had voted "That there be a Free Grammar School at the North end of this Town." [2] In consequence the new committee of inspection was to inspect, not just "the Gram̄er Free School," but all "the Free Grammar Schools." There was still another change of importance that must be noted. The first committee consisted of the ministers and five "Gentlemen, of Liberal Education." The selectmen were substituted for the "Gentlemen" in this committee. For five years this committee of inspection for the grammar school of the town continued to be made up of ministers and selectmen. Then it once more disappeared from the record.[3]

Two years more of gap upon the town records, and again the committee of inspection is revived; and again the revival is accompanied by important changes. In March of 1720/1, the following vote was passed by the town meeting.:

"Voted that the Select men and Such as they Shal desire to Assist them be Inspectors of the Gramer & Wrighting Schools for the year ensuing." [4]

Thus in three establishments of the school inspectors the authority of the committee had occupied different limits. (1) In 1710, it was a committee of the Latin school alone. (2) In

[1] Boston, *Rep. Rec. Com.*, viii., 100.
[2] *Ibid.*, viii., 90.
[3] *Ibid.*, viii., 100, 109, 118, 124, 129.
[4] *Ibid.*, viii., 151.

1714, it was one with authority over both grammar schools. (3) In 1721, it had spread its authority over all the schools, writing schools as well as grammar schools. Henceforth the committee is truly a committee of the town schools in the broadest sense.

Here again there was a change in the denominated membership of the committee of inspection. The ministers as such were no longer made *ex-officio* members of the board of inspection. The matter as to who should accompany the selectmen was now left entirely to the selectmen themselves. Thus, the work of inspection had been done by four differently constituted bodies in four different periods. (1) Prior to 1710, the ministers had been the unofficial visitors of the Latin school. (2) For two years after that date this service had been officially performed by the ministers of the town and five gentlemen of liberal education. (3) From 1714 to 1718, inclusive, the ministers and the selectmen had exercised that function. (4) And finally, after 1721, "the Select men with Such others as they Shal desire to goe with them," became the inspectors of the school.

The form and the function of the town committee on visitation, as fixed by this vote of 1721, continued to be the form and function of the committee that was elected annually from this time until the reorganization of the Boston schools in the year 1789.[1]

Thus the evolution of the Boston committee on school inspection had passed through a preliminary stage of groping after means, as had the Fitchburg committee on the procuring of teachers. This transitional period, beginning with the time the town ceased to leave the matter to the initiative of the ministers, extended over a period of eleven years, from 1710 to 1721. From 1721 on to the reorganization of the school system in 1789, a period of sixty-eight years, an almost unbroken series of records would seem to show that the selectmen and those they chose to assist them performed annually the duty of visiting and inspecting the schools. While the ministers were no longer delegated as an *ex-officio* part of the inspecting committee, they

[1] Boston, *Rep. Rec. Com.*, viii., 151, 162, 171, 181, 188, 194, 203, 217; xii., 4, 14, 20, 28, 39, 78, 104, 111, 126, 129, 153, 183, 187, 188, 209, 212 *et seq.;* xiii., 134 *et seq.;* xiv., 9 *et seq.;* xvi., 10 *et seq.;* xviii., 24 *et seq.;* xxiii., 181 *et seq.;* xxv., 69 *et seq.;* xxvii., 24 *et seq.*

always remained a part of the committee by virtue of the fact that the selectmen, following tradition, continued to invite them to participate along with certain other notables of the town.

While the form and the express function of this town committee of Boston were practically established in the year 1721, the method of performing the function of inspection was not as yet firmly fixed. The details of the record are too meager to tell us how this committee began and continued its service. Here and there, however, some information is given. Careful analysis of such facts as are recorded would seem to show that the committee was far more effective in its earlier years than later, when the significance of the visitation of schools became more and more social and ceremonial, the educational aspect of inspection becoming more and more formal and perfunctory.

In the earlier years there certainly seemed to be more attention given to accomplishing the purpose of the committee, and the committee was evidently used with effectiveness. Within one year of the final re-establishment of the committee, in March of 1721/2, a teacher was actually dismissed upon the report of the inspecting committee. It happened that there had been certain petitions of complaint filed with the town against a Mr. Anger, the master at the South school. The town thereupon "Voted that the Selectmen with Such others as they Shal take with them doe visset the Said School and Enquire into that affair and make Report thereof at the next Geñeal meeting." In the following May the report was presented. It stated that the three gentlemen and the selectmen had "Vissitted the wrighting School at the Southerly End of Boston on Thirsday the 24th apll 1722. and Examined the Scholars under mr Ames Angers Tuition as to their proficiency in Reading writing Scyphering & the masters ability of teaching & Instructing youth & his Rules & methods therfore. And are of Opinion That it will be no Service to the Town to Continue, mr Anger in that Employ."[1] The town immediately sustained the committee's report and discharged the teacher, asking the committee to provide another master.[2] It will be noted that here, as in 1709/10, there is the tendency to give the committee added power, by asking that the committee make provision for a master to succeed the one dismissed.

[1] Boston, *Rep. Rec. Com.*, viii., 164.

[2] *Ibid.*, viii., 165.

The method of inspecting one particular school is suggested in the above report. The general plan of visiting all the schools is not indicated in that report. It is not until 1725 that the plan of procedure is revealed. The following plan was made by the selectmen at a meeting of January 25, 1724/5:

> The Select men agreed to Vizet the Scools upon fryday Next being the 12th. day of february Instant and have agreed to Desire the Revet. messurs Benjamin Wadsworth Joseph Sewall & Samll Checkley ministers to Joyne with them in Vissiting the Schooll of mr. Nathll Williams and to meet at mr. Wadsworths at Two of the Clock & to Desire Coll Tho. fitch & Major Habi Savage to aford their company to vizet the Scholl of mr. Edward Mills & mr Jacib Sheaf at Ten of the Clock in the forenoon and to vizet the North Schools on Tuesday the 23th. at Two of the Clock and the Revr. mesrs. Peter Thatcher, Gee & Calender Presbiters with Thomas & Edward Hutchinson Esqr. & mr. Samll Greenwood to Accompany them.[1]

A day and a half was given over to visitation; the afternoon of the first day to the Latin school or "first Gramer Scholl,"[2] when the selectmen were accompanied by the three ministers only; the morning of the first day to the South and Queens Street writing schools,[3] when the selectmen were accompanied by three citizens; the final half day to the North grammar and the North writing schools,[4] when both ministers and laymen, three of each, attended the selectmen on their duties. The fact that laymen alone accompanied the selectmen when visiting the writing schools, ministers alone when visiting the Latin school, and both laymen and ministers when the tour included both types of schools, seems to bear out the claim that Mr. Martin makes in his *Evolution of the Massachusetts Public School System*, when he says that the Latin schools had been "under the constant and vigilant supervision of the ministers," and that they "regarded this relation not only as a duty but as a right."[5]

The following year the plan was amended so that but one day was occupied by visitation. In consequence, the visitors were divided into two groups instead of three, the North schools being visited by one group and the other two writing schools and the Latin school being visited by the other group. Inasmuch as a grammar school and a writing school was included

[1] Boston, *Rep. Rev. Com.*, xiii., 134.
[2] *Ibid.*, viii., 170.
[3] *Ibid.*, viii., 101.
[4] *Ibid.*, viii., 139.
[5] Martin, *op. cit.*, p. 64.

in each tour, there were both ministers and laymen on each accompanying sub-committee. Different selectmen were assigned to each visitation, all the selectmen not attending as seemed the case before. The Messrs. Hutchinson, donors of the two school-houses "at the North," were named as among the lay visitors to go with the selectmen to the North grammar and writing schools.[1]

In 1727 and 1728, the plan remained substantially the same. Two more laymen and two more selectmen were named on the committee for the three schools in the main part of town. This made three ministers, four laymen, and four selectmen on the committee. The committee for the North schools remained the same—three ministers, three laymen, and three selectmen.[2] Thus all seven selectmen were again visitors of the school.[3]

In December of 1730, the form of the committee which characterized it from that time on was assumed. One committee of three ministers and five gentlemen was invited to make both trips of visitation with the selectmen. With the seven selectmen, this made a total of fifteen visitors. The time of assembly was set at 9 A.M. and 3 P.M. respectively.[4]

The earliest reports of these committees are not obtainable. In the year 1738 a detailed report upon visitation was filed with the town. After having named the seven persons, including the two ministers, who had accompanied the selectmen, the report proceeds to enumerate the number of children in the two grammar and three writing schools. The remainder of the report reads:

> That we heard the Performances of the Lattin Scholars at each Grammar School, And Inspected the Performances of the Scholars in the other Schools, both in Writing and Arithmetick, and heard the younger Scholars read—And that in general they perform'd to the great Satisfaction of the Visitors—And we have grounds to hope that the Masters in the said Several Schools do faithfully Discharge the Trust reposed in them.
>
> And we look upon it as a point of Justice due to the Master of the South Writing School, to Report, that the Writing both of the Master and Scholars has been of late much improved.[5]

So detailed a report is not given very frequently. As time passes, the reports tend to become more formal and less detailed

[1] Boston, *Rep. Rec. Com.*, xiii., 153. *Cf. Ibid.*, viii., 139.
[2] *Ibid.*, xiii., 165, 176.
[3] *Ibid.*, viii., 214; xiii., 176.
[4] *Ibid.*, xiii., 202.
[5] *Ibid.*, viii., 213.

on matters of instruction. The census of school attendance is about the only detail to which attention was given in most of the available reports. The educational work is dismissed with such phrases as "Schools under a good regulation,"[1] "all in good order,"[2] etc. In some cases there is no mention of anything save the census.[3]

There are very good reasons for this. The social aspect of visitation day was constantly growing more dominant, and the committee was increasing in size so as to become unwieldy for efficient use. The social side of the function of visitation begins to become of noticeable importance as early as the year 1733, when the annual dinner of the committeemen and schoolmasters was introduced. In arranging for "visitation day" for the year 1733, a meeting of selectmen, the four ministers, and three laymen who were to accompany the selectmen were named, and immediately thereafter the following vote was passed:

> That a Dinner be provided at Mrs. Wardwells and the above mentioned Gentlemen with the Several Schoolmasters be desired to Dine with us.[4]

Such a dinner evidently became an annual occasion, as it is mentioned the following year,[5] also in 1736,[6] and with considerable consecutiveness thereafter.[7] The custom of having such annual dinner was discontinued, probably for some years, in the Revolutionary period, as the proceedings of a selectmen's meeting in the year 1774 records that "the Selectmen proceeded with the Gentlemen invited to a visitation of the publick Schools; but upon account of the present distress, the Dinner usual on such days was laid aside."[8]

In 1730, when one committee visited all the schools, the number of visitors was only fifteen, including the seven selectmen.[9] In 1741/2, the number had increased to seventeen.[10] In 1751, there were about twenty-seven on the committee, including "the Gentlemen the Representatives of Boston," who appeared as a body among those who accompanied the selectmen.[11] In

[1] Boston, *Rep. Rec. Com.*, xii., 246.
[2] *Ibid.*, xvi., 284.
[3] *Ibid.*, xiv., 308, 309.
[4] *Ibid.*, xiii., 242.
[5] *Ibid.*, xiii., 254.
[6] *Ibid.*, xiii., 302.
[7] *Ibid.*, xxv., 149, 183 *et seq.*
[8] *Ibid.*, xxiii., 222.
[9] *Ibid.*, xiii., 202.
[10] *Ibid.*, xii., 291, 292.
[11] *Ibid.*, xiv., 195, 196.

1755, "the Gentlemen the Overseers of the Poor," twelve in number, helped to swell the total to about thirty-five or more.[1] In 1765, about fifty-three names are listed among the visitors, including "Collo Whiting of Connecticutt."[2] In 1773, the number reached seventy-six, including four strangers from outside the town.[3]

All of them went in procession upon this important day of school visitation. The Governor frequently added dignity to the occasion.[4] The distinguished Representatives and the Overseers of the town added luster, along with the ministers, other citizens and guests from neighboring colonies. And all of them were probably entertained at a dinner given in honor of the occasion, as the records of the selectmen's meetings show the following curious old agreement: "Agreed with Mr. Waort, to dine 70 or 80 Persons in the Day when the Publick Schools are to be visited at 5/ P Man and all the Liquors that shall be drank are to be paid for." This was in 1782.[5] The following year there is a similar memorandum.[6]

In the earlier years, when the visiting committee was small and as yet wieldy, there had been some tendency to give additional powers to this committee, particularly that of hiring teachers. The first visiting committee in 1710 was asked to name a master.[7] In 1722, the committee of visitation which recommended the dismissal of Mr. Anger, was requested to provide another master.[8] With a large committee shifting in its membership, most of the functions came to be performed by the stable nucleus of the committee, the selectmen.[9]

In fact, in certain cases special committees of visitation were at times appointed to supplement the inspection of the larger annual committee, in order that some contingency might be met. In 1729, Mr. Condy, the master of the North writing school, petitioned for an addition to his salary. His petition was referred to the next town meeting, and in the meanwhile a special committee of three, none of them selectmen,[10] were requested "to Inspect the Several Wrighting Schools. . . . And

[1] Boston, *Rep. Rec. Com.*, xiv., 275, 276.

[2] *Ibid.*, xvi., 141, 142.

[3] *Ibid.*, xviii., 129–131.

[4] *Ibid.*, xiv., 9. *Cf.*, *ibid.*, xii., 293; xiv., 98.

[5] *Ibid.*, xxv., 184.

[6] *Ibid.*, xxv., 217.

[7] *Ibid.*, viii., 66.

[8] *Ibid.*, viii., 164.

[9] *Ibid.*, xviii., 252; xxxi., 18.

[10] *Ibid.*, xii., 7.

that they do in an Espesial Mañer Vizit mr Condys School and Report to the Town at their Meeting the Ability and Industry of the said mr Condy and the Proficiency of the Schollers under His Tuition" [1] In 1753, a plea of more assistance from the South writing school led to the appointment of a special committee to investigate and consider the matter.[2] In 1786, one of the masters of the writing schools asks for more assistance, and the selectmen appointed themselves a special committee to visit the school. Upon the basis of this visitation the assistance was granted.[3] In 1788, it was reported to the selectmen that a "few Scholars attend Mr. Davis School for learning Lattin the others attending for learning reading only." At once a committee of three was appointed to visit said school. They reported the statement as entirely groundless.[4]

In the face of the tendency of the committee to become less efficient from an educational standpoint, it is not to be wondered at that an attempt at reform was made. The dissatisfaction must have been considerable about the year 1753, for the town meeting took the matter up and attempted to abolish the existing practice by proposing a new form of committee with smaller membership. It was definitely voted by the town that a committee of seven, "or the Major part of them, be and they are hereby appointed a Committee to Visit the Publick Schools in the Town the Year ensuing at such times as they shall think proper," making report upon the same.[5] But the committee "appeared and pray'd they might be Excus'd from that Service." They were excused, and then it was "Voted, That the Selectmen be & they hereby are desired to Visit the Publick Schools more frequently than has been hitherto Practic'd, and Enquire into the behaviour of the Scholars and the Government and Regulation they are under, and give such Directions to the Masters of said schools concerning them, as they shall judge needful." [6] Later in the year the custom of having the selectmen and others visit was restored by vote of the town meeting.[7] So the reform was short-lived and the committee grew in size and dignity, until a new order of things was established in the year 1789.

[1] Boston, *Rep. Rec. Com.*, xii., 8.
[2] *Ibid.*, xiv., 230, 231.
[3] *Ibid.*, xxv., 317, 318.
[4] *Ibid.*, xxvii., 59, 60.
[5] *Ibid.*, xiv., 231.
[6] *Ibid.*, xiv., 233.
[7] *Ibid.*, xiv., 243.

There is one clause in the instructions to the selectmen that needs to be noticed as it gave the visiting committee a new power. They were not only "to Visit the Publick Schools more frequently," but they were now, also, to "give such Directions to the Masters of said Schools concerning them, as they shall judge needful." Here the visitation and inspection imply more than merely a basis for a report to the town. They imply actual supervision of the teachers and their work, an advance from the position taken in 1710. Then they were merely "to consult and Advise"; now they were to give "Directions." Just how far the power of actual supervision of the teacher's work was attempted cannot be stated. But the principle was recognized, and when a principle is once recognized it is far reaching.

The many successive annual inspecting committees in the town of Boston were distinctly town committees, as the hiring committees of Fitchburg were distinctly organized upon a district basis. It may be said that the movements of the two types of committees were the opposite. The committees on the procuring of teachers started as committees of the whole town, and gradually became bodies of district committeemen. The idea of the inspection committee in Boston started with a single school, spread to the schools of a single grade, then to all the schools. The early town committees of inspection in Boston tended to reflect the district idea in a crude way in the earliest detailed records available, from 1724/5 on, when part of the committee was assigned to the North schools and part to the other schools.[1] This tendency seemed to disappear in the year 1730, when the committee acted as a whole for all the schools.[2]

While the district idea did not reflect itself in the organization of the committee of inspection prior to 1789, the period under discussion, it did begin to reflect itself in school affairs. As the precedent is important, it must be noted. In 1784, a committee "appointed to consider of a future Arangment of the free Schools" reported, and, after bestowing considerable power upon the selectmen, provided for a committee to report a school census to the selectmen.[3] This committee is important, largely because it seems to be the first use of the ward-committee method

[1] Boston, *Rep. Rec. Com.*, xiii., 134, 153, 165.

[2] *Ibid.*, xiii., 202.

[3] *Ibid.*, xxxi., 16–18.

for school purposes in Boston, a method which was later adopted in the next organization of a school committee.

The origin of the ward committee can be traced back to an earlier use of the ward system wherever the duties required the covering of the entire territory of the town to such an extent that a subdivision of the town seemed advisable. Thus, in 1763, the collectors of the taxes were each assigned two wards each.[1] Actual appointments from each ward began in 1768, with the vote "that one Scavinger be chosen out of every Ward." [2] During the Revolutionary War many matters came up that required the use of ward committees, and the precedent seems to have become well established.[3]

The town committee on inspection of schools, as found in Boston, seems to have been the earliest as well as the most important annual committee of its type. It was probably an influence upon other towns, though the absence of inspection and visitation committees from the various town records would seem to indicate that such influence was not very great. The influence of its example upon the legislation of the General Court, which met in the town of Boston, was probably greater. While the idea of an annual inspection committee seemed to develop quite as early in Boston as the movement toward annual committees for the procuring of teachers elsewhere, the general movement, of which the Boston committee was a beginning, was less widespread and later in its development among Massachusetts towns. There are, however, some few instances of other inspection committees which ought to be noted.

In 1744, Cambridge, one of Boston's neighboring towns, elected a committee on the inspection of the "Grammar School." The town record reads as follows:

> Voted, That the Hon. Francis Foxcroft and Saml. Danforth, Esqs., Wm. Brattle, and Edmd. Trowbridge, Esqs., also the Hon. Jona. Remington, Esq., be a committee to inspect the Grammar School in this town, and to inquire (at such times as they shall think meet) what proficiency the youth and children make in their learning. [4]

It is interesting to note that there were no ministers upon this committee as there were upon the Boston committee of the

[1] Boston, *Rep. Rec. Com.*, xvi., 92.

[2] *Ibid.*, xvi., 236, 270; xviii., 155.

[3] *Ibid.*, xviii., 232, 240, 253, 260, 277, 292.

[4] Quoted in Paige, *History of Cambridge*, p. 375.

same period. The committee was in every sense of the word a committee of inspection, with visitation of the schools distinctly implied.

In 1770, the Cambridge committee of inspection was one of nine instead of five as in 1644. There were no ministers mentioned among the nine named upon this committee by the town record. The tendency of inspection committees to gather additional power is well illustrated here. The committee of 1644 was merely "to inspect the Grammar School." This committee was not only "a committee of inspection upon the said schoolmaster," but was also authorized "to chuse a Grammar Schoolmaster," and "empowered to regulate said school." [1]

Almost at the close of the period of the development of committees under the sole sanction of the town governments, the town of Lancaster provided for inspection committees, which were to be joint affairs of the town and the districts. Just about a year before the General Court passed its first law upon the subject of school committees, the town proposed to foster grammar schools, by offering financial support to the "squadron" to the extent of "twelve pounds" a year. Certain conditions had to be observed by the subscribers of the squadron intending to maintain such a school. Among these regulations which were to be observed was one which read as follows:

> 3. The school shall be quarterly visited and inspected by a committee of five persons, whereof the minister of the town for the time being shall be chairman. Two of the four shall be chosen by the town, and two by the squadron. [2]

The minister as an *ex-officio* visitor recurs here as he had in Boston. The most noticeable fact here is, that the committee is not such a town committee as was found in Boston and Cambridge. It was a town committee with two district representatives; in reality a joint committee of the town and squadron.

The precedent of utilizing committees on inspection of schools had been established among the Massachusetts towns through their own initiative. Usually starting as inspection committees of the grammar schools rather than of the elementary

[1] From town record, quoted in Paige, *History of Cambridge*, p. 375.

[2] From town records, quoted in Marvin, *History of Lancaster*, pp. 349, 350.

schools, they tended to be town rather than district committees, for there was seldom more than one grammar school in a town. Usually, because of the long traditional affiliation of the ministers and the higher schools which trained for the ministry, and because the ministers were the one learned class, the ministers were included among the members of the committee on visitation. The power of school inspection, unlike the power of hiring teachers through a committee, was not a power which had been exercised by the town, then by the selectmen, and finally by a regular school committee. It was not a power which had been exercised by the more general authority from the start, and gradually delegated. It was, like certification, a new function for the protection of the town's school, which when it appeared as such was exercised by a special agency largely from the start.

The special agency of the annual visitation and inspection committee, which was evolved by local initiative prior to the year 1789, formed, with the school committee for the provision of teachers, the important precedent of the use of regular school committees in school affairs, a precedent which was later legalized by the state law, and finally made the common practice of all the towns in the Commonwealth.

CHAPTER VIII

SCHOOL COMMITTEES IN THE PERIOD OF STATE LEGISLATION, 1789–1827

Prior to the year 1789, the selectmen of the towns were for the most part charged with the care of matters concerning the schools. In the earliest part of the colonial period various committees, particularly special committees for transient purposes, began to be used. On the precedent and custom established by these, there began to appear in the early eighteenth century certain committees which tended to be elected with increasing regularity, usually each year. There were two types of committees which showed a tendency toward a continued use from year to year. These were the committee for the provision of teachers and the committee for the inspection of the work of the teachers. It was these two types of committees which particularly influenced the general establishment of the school committee under the period of Massachusetts statehood.

In June of 1789, a most important school law of the commonwealth of Massachusetts was passed.[1] It was exceedingly important from the standpoint of the development of the school committee, for it gave existing school committees their first recognition under the state law. The law dealt with two important school functions, certification and inspection. It is the reference to the agencies that were charged with the performance of the two above-named functions that is of particular interest here. The law, in general, placed the responsibility for these duties jointly upon the ministers and the selectmen of the town.

But in each case where the selectmen were mentioned in matters of certification and inspection, it is left optional whether the selectmen or the school committee, if there be one, shall perform such duty. It is in this indirect mention of the school committee that it is given its first legal recognition and its first grant of authority by the state.

In the sections referring to certification of "Preceptors and Teachers of Academies, and all other instructors of youth," after the law had provided for their academic fitness, it provided further that the candidates "shall moreover produce a certificate from a settled minister of the town, district, parish or place, to which such candidate belongs, or from the selectmen of such town or district, or committee of such parish or place," that shall signify his good moral character. When the candidate resided in the town where the school was to have been kept, the certificate of character is waived, but it was "the duty of such Selectmen or Committee, who may be authorized to hire such schoolmaster specially to attend his morals." [2]

In similar sections of the law, relating to the certification of the "master or mistress" of "children in the most early stages of life," the law provided, "That no person shall be allowed to be a master or mistress of such school, or to keep the same, unless he or she shall obtain a certificate from the Selectmen of such town or district where the same may be kept, or the committee appointed by such town, district or plantation to visit

[1] *Acts of 1789*, chap. xix.; (*Perpetual Laws*, ii., 39–44).

[2] *Ibid.*, chap. xix., secs. 4–6.

their schools, as well as from a learned minister settled therein, if such there be." [1]

The same method of reference to the school committee is utilized when the law deals with inspection of schools. The clause provided for the substitution of a school committee for the selectmen. The particular section in point reads:

> And it shall be the duty of the minister or ministers of the gospel and the Selectmen (or such other persons as shall be specially chosen by each town or district for that purpose), of the several towns or districts, to use their influence and best endeavours, that the youth in their respective towns and districts do regularly attend the schools appointed and supported as aforesaid, for their instruction; and once in every six months at least, and as much oftener as they shall determine it necessary, to visit and inspect the several schools in their respective towns and districts, and shall inquire into the regulation and discipline thereof, and the proficiency of the scholars therein, giving reasonable notice of the time of their visitation. [2]

The elements in this law had their foundation in well-established precedent. The minister and selectmen had had previous recognition as school authorities from the state in matters of certification. The minister, as a representative of a learned class with a supposedly natural interest in education, had already established himself in the matter of school inspection. The selectmen had for a long time been the town's representatives in the detailed management of school affairs. Even the incorporation of the committee idea was founded upon existing committees. There are many references in the law to existent committees. Indeed, the references indicate the predominant types of committees that the legislature had in mind. It told what it meant by a committee, by describing the function of such as existed. They were: (1) the "committee, who may be authorized to hire such schoolmaster" [3]; and (2) "the committee appointed by such town, district or plantation to visit their schools." [4] This suggestion of the precedents corresponds exactly with the two types of annual committees which have been found to be most conspicuous in the preceding period.

While the act was founded upon precedent in the matter of the powers and agencies with which it concerned itself, it was

[1] *Acts of 1789*, chap. xix., sec. 10.
[2] *Ibid.*, chap. xix., sec. 8.
[3] *Ibid.*, chap. xix., sec. 6.
[4] *Ibid.*, chap. xix., sec. 10.

distinctly a constructive act. It made the inspection of schools a general requirement, as it had previously done with certification, thus guaranteeing an investigation into the teacher's ability not only before he had commenced to teach, but also during the period of engagement.

The law was constructive, inasmuch as it was a large influence upon the projection of the committee idea in the regulation of schools.[1] While this act was exceedingly indirect in its treatment of the whole committee idea, it was very influential. It did more than to sanction the committee, thus encouraging their organization in towns which had none. It placed further obligations upon the selectmen, intensifying the very conditions which had made necessary the delegation of authority which had usually been exercised by selectmen to special and continuous school committees. The nature of the function of visitation itself was conducive to the use of the committee, more than if the burden imposed had been of a different nature. The new duty of visitation and inspection had, from the beginning of the century, been associated with the committee idea. The school committee was the traditional machinery for visitation. Hence it was the means most likely to be used in putting the law into effect in the towns.

The very vagueness of the law would suggest that there were many variations in the manner with which the law operated in the various towns, each of which could, to a certain extent, make its own interpretation of the law within certain broad limits. This was actually the case. In consequence, the influence of the law may be best observed by a study of the individual towns.

Since the law recognized two existing types of committees, the town committee on inspection and the committee on hiring of teachers which reflected the district system, and permitted certification and inspection by committees consisting of such "persons as shall be specially chosen by each town or district for that purpose,"[2] it will be necessary to note changes occurring

[1] The committee idea was further stimulated by a statute of the General Court which had to do with the building of schoolhouses rather than with their internal management. An act of 1800 (Mass., *Perpetual Laws*, ii., 80) empowered districts "to choose a Committee to superintend the building and repairing" of schoolhouses.

[2] *Acts of 1789*, chap. xix., sec. 8.

subsequent to this act in three types of communities. These are, namely: (1) Those having town committees on inspection of schools; (2) those having committees on the providing of teachers and reflecting the district organization; and (3) those having no regular school committees and organizing them for the first time under this act.

Of the few towns having annual committees on inspection of schools, Boston was by far the most important. It had been the earliest in the establishment of the idea and the longest in its use, so far as the records show. It was one of the first towns in the commonwealth to respond to the demands of the new law. The act was passed June 25, 1789.[1] In September of 1789, it seems that a large number of the inhabitants had proposed a reform of the existing system of schools, and that certain definite propositions were made. The propositions were then "referred to a Committee of Twelve persons to be chosen out of each Ward."[2] In October the committee presented its report, which was amended and accepted by the town.[3] It provided for a new arrangement and regulation of schools. There were to be one Latin grammar, three writing, and three reading schools, which were to be under the regulation of a "Visiting Committee."

That part of the resolution on the topic of schools which concerns the school committee is as follows:

> That the Committee be annually chosen by ballot to consist of twelve in addition to the Selectmen, whose business it shall be to Visit the Schools once in every Quarter, and as much oftener at they shall Judge proper with three of their number at least, to consult together in order to devise the best Methods for the Instruction & Government of the Schools and to communicate the result of their determinations to the Masters; to determine at what hours the Schools shall begin, and to appoint play Days in their Visitations, to enquire into the particular regulations of the Schools both in regard to Instruction & Discipline, and give such advice to the Masters as they shall think proper, to examine the Scholars in the particular branches which they are taught, and by all proper Methods to excite in them a Laudable ambition to excel in a virtuous, amiable deportment and in every branch of useful knowledge.[4]

By this reform the whole constitution of the inspection committee of Boston had been changed. A relatively small com-

[1] *Acts of 1789*, chap. xix.
[2] Boston, *Rep. Rec. Com.*, xxxi., 205, 206.
[3] *Ibid.*, xxxi., 208, 209.
[4] *Ibid.*. xxxi., 209.

mittee of the selectmen and twelve others had been substituted for a large and unwieldy visitation committee of eighty or ninety, which could not have been efficient so long as it was so large and so completely dominated by the festive and social aspect of visitation day.

The twelve men were now chosen from wards of the city by the town meeting, instead of from the whole town by the selectmen as before. In a sense this might be considered as an influence of the district system, operating where the district could not have been so important as it was in more remote places where population was more scattered. Its origin and its earliest use in school affairs have already been indicated. It was used in 1784, when the census takers were appointed, two from each ward.[1] It was used in 1789, when the committee on reform of the schools, which recommended the appointment of a ward committee to act with the selectmen as a school committee, was itself appointed by wards.[2] As the ward system persisted in Boston for a long period of time it needs to be noted at this point.

The town of Boston had not only observed the provisions of the new law with regard to the visitation of schools, but had lain down requirements in advance of those in the state law. Visitation was required at least quarterly instead of once in every six months. Whereas the law authorized committees to "inquire into the regulation and discipline thereof, and the proficiency of the scholars therein," the Boston committee was given the additional power of supervising the masters. They were "to devise the best Methods for the Instruction & Government of the Schools and to communicate the result of their determinations to the Masters," and after visitation "give such advice to the Masters as they shall think proper." Here then there appeared a school committee with full supervisory powers over the teacher. It was more than a committee of inspection. It was a committee of inspection and supervision.

Four months later, in February of 1790, the final step was taken which made the Boston committee, at least as regards function, a school committee in the modern sense, a committee in which is centered all the main functions of school administration and school supervision. In that month "the Commission

[1] Boston, *Rep. Rec. Com.*, xxxi., 18, 19. [2] *Ibid.*, xxxi., 218, 219.

given to the School Committee on the 15th of October last" was explained by the following sweeping vote:

> Voted that the Committee of twelve appointed in October last to manage in concert with the Selectmen the affairs & government of the Schools, be authorized with the Selectmen in future to exercise all the powers relating to the Schools & School Masters, which the Selectmen or such Committees are authorized by the Laws of this state or the Votes of this town to exercise, any former Votes of the Town notwithstanding. [1]

The first committee was elected in October, 1789. Three of the first twelve were ministers.[2] The committee was again elected in February, 1790,[3] and each year thereafter. With each election of the committee, there was the vote of a resolution similar to that given in 1790, authorizing "the aforegoing Committee who conjunctly are to be termed the School Committee . . . . to manage and regulate the affairs & government of the Schools, and in future to exercise all the Powers relating to the Schools & School Masters." [4]

In 1822, when Boston became a city, the status of the school committee was somewhat changed as to membership and method of election. Section 19 of the special act of incorporation provided as follows:

> And the said citizens shall, at the same time, and in like manner,[5] elect one person in each ward, to be a member of the School Committee, for the said city; and the persons so chosen, shall jointly with the Mayor and Alderman, constitute the School Committee for the said city, and have the care and superintendence of the public schools. [6]

With this special act of incorporation Boston was removed from the influence of general acts regulating the school committee and its powers and, after the manner of specially incorporated cities, developed its school system largely under its own charter.

In Cambridge, one of the towns which had also had a com-

[1] Boston, *Rep. Rec. Com.*, xxxi., 215.

[2] *Ibid.*, xxxi., 211.

[3] *Ibid.*, xxxi., 218, 219.

[4] *Ibid.*, xxxi., pp. 245, 246, 280, 281, 287, 288, 320, 351, 420.

[5] The election of school committeemen was done at the respective ward meetings of the citizens. *Act of February 23, 1822*, sec. 19.

[6] *Act of Feb. 23, 1822*, sec. 19. There were at this time twelve wards (*ibid.*, sec. 2), and eight aldermen (*ibid.*, sec. 6).

mittee on inspection of schools, no very great change in plan was made. It is not known whether or not the inspection committee of which there is evidence in 1744 and 1770 was constantly maintained. At any rate, in the year 1795, a committee of seven, including three ministers, was "chosen for the purpose of superintending the schools in this town, and carrying into effect the School Act."[1] The beginning of the use of the word "superintending" is to be noted.

Lancaster, which had made some provision for an inspection committee in 1788,[2] continued to maintain such in some form. In 1793, the committee "to inspect schools" seemed to be one of three.[3] In 1794, it was one of seven, including the minister.[4] In 1798 and 1799, the committee was one of eleven, of which the minister was an *ex-officio* member.[5] In 1801, there were eleven districts and a committee of twelve on visitation, with the minister as a member, which would lead one to believe that the hiring committee for the district schools, with the minister added as an *ex-officio* member, had been made the town committee on inspection of schools for a number of years past.[6] This seems to be further corroborated by the fact that special committees were called into requisition to get masters for the singing school and Latin school in the years 1799 and 1801, respectively.[7]

The towns mentioned suggest how varied were the methods used in forming inspection committees under the new law of 1789 in three different towns which had already established the idea of inspection committees prior to 1789. Cambridge maintains its committee as a town committee. So does Boston, but the method of choice is one of ward selection. Lancaster, under the influence of the district system to a greater extent, makes a town inspection committee by adding the minister to its district committee. Yet in each case the necessity of visiting all the town schools made the committees town committees rather than district or ward committees.

Just what effect the demand for town school inspection had upon those communities, in which annual committees for the providing of teachers had existed, is now to be determined. Fitchburg, which had had a district committee of six for this purpose in

[1] Paige, *History of Cambridge*, p. 376.
[2] Marvin, *History of Lancaster*, p. 349.
[3] *Ibid.*, p. 354.
[4] *Ibid.*, p. 355.
[5] *Ibid.*, pp. 356, 357.
[6] *Ibid.*, p. 400.
[7] *Ibid.*, pp. 357, 400.

1789,[1] continued its district committeemen as before, but added one more committeeman the following year, as it had added one more district.[2] In fact, with the year 1790, the committee, the district having been sanctioned by law,[3] became professedly a district committee. A town vote of this year declared "that there shall be a Committee man Choose to each Destrict yearly they to be under the Directions of the Destrict they belong."[4] The committee seems to have remained one of seven until 1798, when increased activity regarding the schools led to the redistricting of the town into ten and then eleven districts, and the formation of district school committees of one for each district.[5] In 1811, a district was divided and this increased the district committee to twelve, at which number it usually remained until at least 1827, when the matter of district committees was treated by state law.[6]

Nothing appears to have been done in the matter of appointing a special committee for examining the schools until the year 1808. In that year such a committee was voted. It was to "consist of Eleven," the same number as the annual hiring committee, thus reflecting the dominance of the district idea even in the matter of examining the town's schools. Two of this committee were ministers. It was further "Voted that the Committee be requested to attend the schools when they begin & at the time of closing the schools."[7] The time stated for visitation is interesting, inasmuch as the beginning and the ending weeks of school were later made the express time for visitation by state statute. It is probable that the shortness of school terms among the district schools made visitation in accordance with such order fall within the time of six months set by law.

The influence of the district system upon the town inspection committee was transient. It lasted but the single year. The following year, 1809, the committee consisted of five members for the town.[8] It was the same in 1810,[9] and continued

[1] Fitchburg, *Records*, ii., 20.

[2] *Ibid.*, ii., 45.

[3] *Acts of 1789*, chap. xix., secs. 1, 2.

[4] Fitchburg, *Records*, ii., 45.

[5] *Ibid.*, ii., 59, 67, 90, 111, 145, 146, 174; iv., 8, 116, 130, 143, 144.

[6] *Ibid.*, v., 37, 40, 41 *et seq.* In 1814, there were fourteen committeemen. No reason for the change is evident. (*Ibid.*, v., 84.)

[7] *Ibid.*, iv., 378.

[8] *Ibid.*, iv., 406.

[9] *Ibid.*, v., 40.

at that number annually thereafter, through the year 1813.[1] Beginning with the year 1811, the election of the five persons to attend specially to the matter of inspection is spoken of as an enlargement or addition to the existing school committee which was a district committee. In 1811, the election of the district committee was followed by these votes of the town meeting: "Voted that the school committee be inlarged"; "Voted that five be added to the committee."[2] Similar votes are recorded in 1812 and 1813.[3] Both of these additions included clergymen in accordance with the stipulation of the law. The idea of enlargement seems to bear with it the implication that the district committeemen also visited the schools. After 1813, the special annual inspection committee of five seems to have disappeared[4] until its revival in 1826, as a result of the state legislation of that year.[5] This does not imply that there was no inspection of schools during this period. The existing district committeemen and the ministers might have performed that duty. This would have met the requirements of the law of 1789. There is, however, no evidence to show what was actually done.

The town of Grafton, which had a school committee for the providing of teachers in the district schools prior to the year 1789, continued its district committee annually through the period under study. It was a committee of nine from 1787 to 1796, inclusive.[6] From 1797 to 1812, inclusive, it was one of ten members.[7] After that time it was a committee of nine again.[8] There seems to be no evidence of a special committee on inspection, as was found in Fitchburg. If the town obeyed the law, the duty was performed jointly by the ministers and the selectmen or district committee.

The towns of Fitchburg and Grafton, representing communities in which there were existing school committees, of the district type, give us two distinct methods of obeying the law. In the case of Fitchburg, a separate town inspection committee, was brought into existence along side of the district committee for the providing of teachers. In the case of Grafton no new agency was devised. Even in Fitchburg the town committee tended to

[1] Fitchburg, *Records*, v., 30, 45, 70.
[2] *Ibid.*, v., 30.
[3] *Ibid.*, v., 45, 70.
[4] *Ibid.*, 84 *et seq.*
[5] *Ibid.*, v., 288, 292.
[6] Pierce, *History of Grafton*, p. 424.
[7] *Ibid.*, pp. 424, 425.
[8] *Ibid.*; pp. 425, 426.

become merged with the district committee and finally disappeared, leaving the district committee as the only committee on schools for about thirteen years.

Among the towns which established school committees of one sort or another for the first time during this period, many variations are found. They may be grouped roughly into three classes: (1) Those that commenced with a joint committee, of which the town selectmen were still officially a part; (2) those that commenced with a special inspection and certification committee; and (3) those that commenced with the district committee for the providing of teachers, and used it in connection with the ministers for other purposes.

While the committee movement had gained much sway in certain places rather early in the eighteenth century, there were some other places where the selectmen were still charged with the responsibility for schools. Certain of these responded to the demand for inspection and certification agencies by calling the existing authorities "the school committee." Thus the selectmen were officially joined with the ministers by town vote and called the school committee. Sometimes the committee was enlarged so as to include persons whose membership was not *ex-officio*.

In 1789, the town of Marlborough, taking cognizance of the act of the General Court, appointed a committee to consider the same and report to the town. In January of 1790 the committee reported the following decision: "that the Selectmen for the time being, be a committee to provide a school-master duly qualified to keep said schools, as the said Act directs." [1] This represents little advance from the condition before the law. It is some advance inasmuch as the selectmen are recognized as performing their school duties as a chosen school committee rather than as town selectmen.

In 1803, the advance from the use of selectmen to district school committeemen, which was characteristic where the provision of teachers was a matter demanding attention, was made. At that time there was appointed "a Committee of seven persons, one for each school-house," whose duty it was to "provide suitable school mistresses . . . and regulate said woman schools according to their discretion." [2]

[1] Hudson, *History of Marlborough*, pp. 215, 216. [2] *Ibid.*, pp. 217, 218

The town of Wenham presents a somewhat interesting method of meeting the demands of the law of 1789. The law had provided for the exercise of the duty of visitation by the ministers and the selectmen or committee. This particular town did not accept the option in the matter of selectmen or committee. It established both the existing committee and the selectmen as part of the committee, with the ministers. In 1806, the town voted as follows:

"That the selectmen and the committee, chosen in each school ward for procuring schoolmasters for the time being, shall be a committee for the purpose of visiting schools with Rev. R. Anderson, for the better management of schools agreeable to law."[1]

Just how the matter of certification was attended to is not shown.

The town of Oxford presented a similar situation in 1810. In that year the committee for visitation and regulation of schools consisted of ministers, selectmen, and a special committee of three. This is indicated by the report of the committee for that year. Since the report is of interest as indicating the attitude of the people of one community in the matter of school inspection, as well as showing the constitution of the committee, it may be quoted somewhat fully. It is as follows:

1st your committee in company with the Rev'd Josiah Moulton and the Gentlemen Selectmen of sd Town have attended their Duty and find the several Schools with the exception of Mr. Harwood's ward, viz., No 2, in a flourishing State being Surplyd with Able Teachers and Actuated with a Laudable Ambition to Excell—the reason of your committee's making an Exception of Mr. Harwood's ward is that a large part of the Parents and Guardians in sd ward are opposed to haveing there schools Inspected and Keep there children at home, which Practice in the Opinion of your Committee is very Injurious as it tends to Sap the first principals in Society and frustrate every necessary regulation.[2]

The town of Hanover likewise utilized the selectmen as part of a special school committee. In 1812, the three selectmen and the three ministers were chosen as a school committee.[3] In 1819, special school committeemen, having no other official function, were added to the committee. Early in the year, a

[1] Allen, *History of Wenham*, pp. 114, 115.
[2] Daniels, *History of Oxford*, pp. 772, 773.
[3] Barry, *History of Hanover*, p. 91.

school committee, consisting of "the three selectmen, and all the ministers in the town, together with" six others, was named.[1] This was in March. In November of the same year the above committee was discharged and a new committee appointed. This committee omitted the selectmen, naming five citizens of the community, of which number three were ministers and one a doctor.[2] In the three committees named at different times within this one town, there is indicated a distinct evolution. The first committee is entirely *ex-officio*. The second consists of six persons beside the ministers and selectmen, named as such. The third is a committee of five persons rather than officers, three of which are at the same time ministers.

In the case of the three towns just treated, the selectmen were, in the beginning at least, an integral part of the first school committees. In other towns the start was made at once with committees of one type or another, of which the selectmen were not an official part. Some towns started with a special town inspection and certification committee; others started with the district committee for the hiring of teachers.

Brookline, near neighbor of Boston, was one of the first towns which started the establishment of a regular school committee of the town committee-of-inspection type. At a meeting of July 25, 1791, the following vote was recorded:

> "The Rev'd Joseph Jackson, William Aspinwall, Esq'r and Mr. John Goddard were chosen to Examin the Schools on the last Wednesday in Octob'r Next, and on the last Wednesday in Every Quarter through the year." [3]

It is difficult to say whether or not this was a committee which was elected annually or served at the pleasure of the town. The latter seems most probable, since the only traces of appointments to this committee indicated on the town records up to the year 1823 occur when vacancies were filled.[4] In 1823, the town passed the special vote, "That the School committee be Elected Annually at March Meeting." [5]

From the year 1809, on, three men were annually "chosen a committee to provide School Mistresses," for the "Three womans schools" of the "summer Season Viz one in the North District

[1] Barry, *History of Hanover*, p. 91.
[2] *Ibid.*, p. 91.
[3] Brookline, *Records*, i., 379.
[4] *Ibid.*, i., 400, 458, 497, 520.
[5] *Ibid.*, i., 548.

one in the South district and one in the Middle district."[1] Thus the committee for providing teachers for the district schools came to exist by the side of the town inspection committee.

In 1823, at the same meeting at which it was decided to elect the school committee annually, it was also "Voted That the School committee have a joint power with the Selectmen in Regulating the Schools."[2] It is difficult to know whether it was a step forward or a step backward. As an increase of power, it was the former, as the committee was now to regulate as well as to inspect the schools. The reversion to the use of the selectmen, conjointly with the committee, was in a sense a reversion to a former agency for school control.

The town of Northfield was another community which proceeded to the use of the town inspection committee after the law of 1789. Sometime in the year 1800, it established a committee of seven persons, among which was the minister of the town. The purpose of this committee was "to inspect the schools of the town."[3]

Palmer was still another community which started the same way. In 1805, a committee of five was named "to inspect all the schools in the town of Palmer."[4] In 1807, the committee was one of three members only.[5] In 1811, two types of committees were named. The inspection committee was broadened so as to be a committee on examination and certification of teachers as well. In addition to this committee there was also recorded the election of a district committee, for "one man in each school district was chosen to employ school masters & set up the schools." There were three on the first named committee and nine on the last.[6]

In the following year, 1812, a still further differentiation was made. Three committees were provided. The minister was made a committee of one to examine masters; there was a district committee of eight to select masters; and, finally, there was a committee of five to examine the schools.[7]

Most of the towns which started with the committee idea

[1] Brookline, *Records*, i., 488, 489, 497, 501, 506, 511, 519, 525, 530 *et seq.*

[2] *Ibid.*, i., 548.

[3] Sheldon & Temple, *History of Northfield*, pp. 353, 354.

[4] Temple, *History of Palmer*, p. 294.

[5] *Ibid.*, p. 294.

[6] *Ibid.*, p. 294.

[7] *Ibid.*, p. 294.

seemed to start from the idea of the district committee for providing teachers and schools. It has already been indicated that the spontaneous movement tending towards the annual hiring committee was somewhat stronger than that tending towards the annual committee of inspection. The same causes for this fact would operate after 1789. In fact, the recognition of the district system by the law of 1789 [1] only added force to the district school committee movement, by encouraging more district schools, and therefore the need of more teachers for such increased number of small schools. The tendency, therefore, in spite of the demand for inspection and certification, was very strong in the direction of committees for providing teachers, which could also be utilized under the law for inspection as legally as any special committee named for that purpose.

Douglas was one of the towns that appointed district committees and gave them regulative power. In 1790, a committee of three persons in each district was appointed to "set up and regulate schools." There were ten districts in the town at this time, and therefore thirty committeemen.[2] The district form of the committee in this case had taken a form which practically made ten district committees of three each. In the other cases that have been noticed, where one from each district was a member, the term "committee" was as frequently used as the term "committees."

In 1792, the town of Tisbury was divided into four districts, and there was appointed a committee of three for each district to "be a Committee to Provide A Schoolmaster and an House to keep a School in." [3] In 1797, the warrant stated the function of the committee to be appointed as follows: "And also to Choose Committees in the Several School districts in Sd town to provide masters for each destrict and to Superentend the Same." One committeeman was chosen for the first and third districts and two for the second and fourth.[4] The various committeemen for each district seemed to vary in number and distribution from this time on.[5]

The precinct of North Brookfield, which for all practical purposes managed its affairs as a town, chose a committee of seven

[1] *Acts of 1789*, chap. xix., secs. 1, 2.

[2] Emerson, *History of Douglas*, pp. 90, 91.

[3] Tisbury, *Records*, pp. 285, 286.

[4] *Ibid.*, p. 305.

[5] *Ibid.*, 311 *et seq.*

"to provide and take care of the several Schools in the Precinct." This was in 1792.[1] In 1795, it was a committee of eight.[2] It is altogether probable that this was a district committee, as were the other committees for the provision of teachers, for in 1805 the district system asserted itself in a manner which is of considerable interest. The state later incorporated the same power in the general law of the state.[3] It was voted by the town, "To relinquish the right of choosing School Committee-men, and leave it to each district to appoint its own."[4] In 1809, however, the town or precinct reassumed the appointment of district committeemen.[5]

In 1795, the town of Northampton, much after the manner of Boston in 1789, had a committee for the purpose of reporting a plan of education. It was with the report of this committee that a general school committee came into existence. Its general supervisory power was indicated by a paragraph in the report, which reads as follows:

> That it shall be the duty of the School Committee to provide Instructors, to apportion the Scholars to the different Schools, to determine on School houses, to alter if they see fit the time and manner of instructing Girls, and in General, to inspect & regulate the Schools according to their best discretion.[6]

This committee evidently grew out of the need "to provide Instructors," which is the first mentioned duty in this report of functions. In 1810, the members of the school committee were appointed from each district.[7] As committees on provision of teachers were usually district committees, this would seem to bear out the statement as to the cause of the committee.

While the town of Weston had not developed an annual school committee prior to the year 1789, it had used the committee idea to a considerable extent.[8] In 1796, it began to elect such committee by recording the following vote: "Voted that the following Persons be Committees, to Provide

[1] Temple, *History of North Brookfield*, p. 256.

[2] *Ibid.*, p. 256.

[3] *Acts of 1827*, chap. cxliii., sec. 6. In the appointment of district prudential committeemen, the town could permit each district to elect its own.

[4] Temple, *op. cit.*, p. 256.

[5] *Ibid.*, p. 256.

[6] Trumbull, *History of Northampton*, p. 566.

[7] *Ibid.*, p. 588.

[8] Weston, *Records*, i., 50 *et seq.*

Schoolmasters in the Districts to which they respectively belong." Six district committees of three each were named. Among the members of the third committee named was the Rev. Sam'l Kendall, minister of the town.[1] The appearance of a minister on this committee indicates a fact which has not been noticed before in connection with district committees for the providing of teachers.

These six committees of three each were elected each succeeding year until the year 1826, when an important change was made.[2] There seems to have been no special response to the law of 1789 by the creation of special means to meet its demands until the year 1806. It was then "Voted also to choose two persons to be a committee with the Revd. Samuel Kendall to examine all persons who may offer themselves as instructors of schools—Doctor Amos Bancroft & Isaac Fiske chosen."[3] It can be readily understood why the first committee other than the district committee should have been one on certification instead of inspection. The six committees of three each could visit schools with the minister, but they were far too bulky a means for the purpose of examining candidates. Hence, if the selectmen were not to be brought into utilization again, against the now well-established precedent of using school committees for school purposes, a smaller committee was necessary.

Under the law of 1789, the movement tending toward the use of regular committees in the management of school affairs grew. The towns which had had committees made further development of them for the purposes laid down by the General Court. Others created committees. Sometimes the committee on inspection came to inherit all the powers of school management usually given to delegated authority as in the case of Boston. Sometimes, as in the case of Tisbury, the district committeemen for hiring teachers proceeded to superintend the schools. Again, as in Brookline, an inspection committee and a committee on providing schoolmistresses were maintained side by side. In the case of Weston, the committee existing alongside of the committee on teachers was the certification committee instead of the inspection committee. In Palmer, for a short period, there were three committees at one time, for the pur-

[1] Weston, *Records*, i., 467.

[2] *Ibid.*, i., 475 *et seq.;* ii., 8 *et seq.*

[3] *Ibid.*, ii., 32.

poses, respectively, of certification, inspection, and provision of teachers. The variation existed not only as to the number of coexisting committees, their functions, and their origin, but likewise as to the number of persons upon a given committee and the method of selecting them. The personnel of certain committees was largely *ex-officio*. Other committees were made up of others than existing town officials. While most all committees were elected by the town, many committees were named so as to correspond with and be representative of the various school districts. In some cases the town might go so far as to allow the district to select its own committee, as in the case of North Brookfield. Other committees, again, were distinctly town committees. The variation was wide, and it is not surprising that the state soon proceeded to legislate some uniformity.

And the state could legislate certain uniformity upon the basis of certain broad tendencies in the direction of uniformity to be observed amidst all the variations. There was certainly coming to be a more widespread use of the school committee for school purposes. The membership of such committees, where the law allowed communities to express themselves, as in the case of selectmen, became less and less an *ex-officio* membership. Then, there was a strong tendency for committees of inspection not only to become certificating and hiring committees, but committees for the "general charge and superintendence of all the public schools." There is a very noticeable tendency during this period for towns to describe the functions of committees in such terms as "to take care of," "regulate," and "superintend" the schools. As a result, in 1826 the General Court began its work of establishing some uniformity in the application of committee government to all the schools of the state.

The act of 1826 established the town school committee as a permanent part of the Massachusetts school system. It required that each town in the commonwealth should have an annual school committee of at least five persons, who should assume the general charge and superintendence of the public schools. They were specifically given the functions of school inspection, certification, the prescribing of school texts, and the making of an annual report on school affairs to the Secretary of the commonwealth.[1] Neither minister nor selectman was given

[1] *Acts of 1826*, chap. clxx.

any place upon the school committee by virtue of his official position.

The most important part of this law, section one, read as follows:

That each town in this Commonwealth, shall, at the annual March or April meeting, choose a School Committee, consisting of not less than five persons, who shall have the general charge and superintendence of all the public schools in said town; and it shall be the duty of said committee, to visit the schools in said town, which are kept through the year, at least once a quarter, for the purpose of making a careful examination of the same, and to see that the scholars are properly supplied with books; also, to inquire into the regulation and discipline of such schools, and the proficiency of the scholars therein; and it shall also be the duty of said committee to visit each of the district schools in said town, for the purposes aforesaid, on some day during the first week of the commencement thereof, and also on some day during the last two weeks of the same; and it shall further be the duty of one or more of said committee to visit all the schools in the town, at least once a month, for the purposes aforementioned, without giving previous notice thereof to the instructors. And it is hereby further made the duty of said committee, to require full and satisfactory evidence of the good character and qualifications of said instructors, conformably to the laws now in force relating to the subject; or to require them to furnish such other evidence of character and qualifications, as shall be equally satisfactory to said committee; and no instructor shall be entitled to receive any compensation for his service, who shall teach any of the schools aforesaid, without first obtaining from said committee a certificate of his fitness to instruct.[1]

It will be noticed that one important power, that of providing the teacher, is nowhere specifically assigned to the town committee. This authority had for a long time, among a great many communities, been exercised by committees made up of men representing the various school districts. The matter of having a school in each section or district of the town with a teacher chosen by a person or by persons representative of the district, had come to be regarded as a right of the district. The law had recognized one committee movement in the law of 1826, but it had not recognized the other committee movement, the one which had been associated with the district and the hiring of the district school teacher, a movement which had manifested a more spontaneous and widespread growth than had the movement for a committee with certain powers of super-

[1] *Acts of 1826*, chap. clxx., sec. 1.

vision. That recognition had soon to come. It came in the following year.

The act of 1827 was a most important school document.[1] It was the most lengthy school act passed by the General Court up to that time. It entered into the detail of school control and management of schools as no act had done before. So far as the town school committee was concerned, it practically re-enacted the law of 1826 with certain detailed changes.

The size of the town committee on schools was changed from "not less than five persons" to "three, five or seven persons. . . . Provided that any town, containing four thousand inhabitants, and upwards, may choose an additional number, not exceeding five." [2]

In the matter of certification of teachers, it was now explicitly stated that the school committee might "satisfy themselves, by personal examination or otherwise, of their literary qualifications and capacity for the government of schools." [2]

There was some slight change in the matter of visitation and inspection of schools also. Before, the whole committee was required to visit the yearly or town school at least each quarter, and the district schools at the beginning and close. With the new law, only "some one or more of them" were required to visit the district schools. The visit at the beginning of the term might be made any day in the first two weeks instead of some day in the first week. [2]

Certain limitations were also imposed in the matter of changing class books. Where books still fit for use were not "extremely faulty," and which were "possessed in such numbers as to admit of the proper and convenient classification of the school," they were not to be put aside for other books without "the consent of the parents, masters, or guardians of a majority of the children, so already provided" for a term of two years. The adoption of books favoring "any particular sect or tenet" was forbidden.[3]

Additional power was specifically given to the town school committee in the matter of admitting the children to schools intended for the use of the whole town. It amounted to power

[1] *Acts of 1827*, chap. cxliii.
[2] *Ibid.*, chap. cxliii., sec. 5.
[3] *Ibid.*, chap. cxliii., sec. 7.

in the matter of grading the schools to a certain extent. The law stated that "it shall further be the duty of said committee to determine the number and qualifications of the scholars, to be admitted to the school kept for the use of the whole town."[1]

While these specific changes were made, there was no very significant change from the nature and purpose of the committee as it was laid down in the act of 1826. The broad powers laid down in that first act were maintained in the act of the following year.

The most important feature of the act of 1827 was the requirement of towns that they shall elect prudential committee-men from each district in the town, who shall have the power to "provide schooling," that is, to "select and contract with a school teacher for his own district" and "to provide a suitable place for the school of the district." This was practically a requirement of each town that it shall elect such a committee as was found in Fitchburg during the eighteenth century.

The section of the act which provided for a district prudential committee is as follows:

> Be it further enacted, That each town in this Commonwealth, which is or may be divided into school districts, at their annual meeting aforesaid, shall, in addition to the committee aforesaid, choose a committee for each school district in said town, consisting of one person, who shall be a resident in the district for which he shall be chosen, and be called the prudential committee thereof, whose duty it shall be to keep the school house of such district in good order, at the expense of such district; and in case there be no school house, to provide a suitable place for the school of the district, at the expense thereof; to provide fuel, and all things necessary for the comfort of the scholars therein; to select and contract with a school teacher for his own district, and to give such information and assistance to the said school committee, as may be necessary to aid them in the discharge of the duties required of them by this act: Provided, that in any town in this Commonwealth, which shall so determine, the members of said prudential committee may be chosen in the several school districts to which they respectively belong, in such manner as said district may decide.[2]

A penalty upon the town was also imposed in this law, not only for failure to elect "a school committee to superintend said schools," but likewise, "if said town is divided into school

[1] *Acts of 1827*, chap. cxliii., sec. 5. [2] *Ibid.*, chap. cxliii., sec. 6.

districts" for failure to choose "prudential committees in the several districts."[1]

Thus, after almost two centuries of life, the commonwealth of Massachusetts had evolved specialized means for the control of the public schools. Out of the temporary committees of the seventeenth and early eighteenth centuries, two types of annual committees had evolved. In certain communities, the town committee for the visitation and inspection of schools was used. In certain other communities, more numerous perhaps, the annual committee for the providing of schools and teachers, a committee that reflected the district system to a considerable extent, was the type used. Recognizing these two committees as established precedents, the state sanctioned their use by the towns which had chosen or might chose to use them. Under the sanction of this law the movement toward the increased use of the school committee quickened and broadened. Finally, the state, in 1826, made a town committee for the general charge and superintendence of the schools a compulsory matter. In 1827, it made the same demand in the matter of district committees for the provision of teachers and schools.

Thus was the school committee idea made an integral part of the Massachusetts school system. Step by step the control of the schools had passed from the direct control of the town-meeting to the indirect control of the town through some delegated authority. Selectmen, as the official representatives of the town, and ministers, as the best representatives of the learned class, were called into requisition. But as the functions of school management and school supervision became more and more numerous and more and more complex, the demand for a special school authority, unburdened by other cares, increased. The town school committee and the district prudential committee were the result. The former was destined to a long and continuous existence as an agency for school supervision; the latter was destined to live as long as the district system and no longer.[2]

[1] *Acts of 1827*, chap. cxliii., sec. 19.

[2] The town committee for "the general charge and superintendence of the schools" exists to-day (*Mass. Revised Laws*, chap. xlii., sec. 27). The district prudential committee ceased to exist with the final passing of the district system, which was in 1882 (Martin, *op. cit.*, p. 205).

CHAPTER IX

THE POWERS OF THE SCHOOL COMMITTEES

With the year 1827, the General Court of the commonwealth of Massachusetts had established the district and town school committees as integral parts of the machinery for the management, care, and supervision of town and district schools. The functions of these committees were laid down with considerable definiteness. They had been exercised through the preceding centuries, directly or by implication, by various agencies, until they had finally come to be the duties of the school committees. The more definite and important of these powers, the development of which has been in a degree indicated in the previous chapters, were: (1) the appointment of teachers, (2) the certification of teachers, (3) the visitation and inspection of class-room work, (4) the direction and supervision of the teachers' work, (5) the adoption of text-books, and (6) the classification of pupils.

The committees enjoyed other powers, as did the town-meeting. The matter of support was primarily the business of the latter, and continues to be so to the present time.[1] The prudential committee might "provide a suitable place for the school," provide fuel and other necessary things for the conduct of the school in their own particular district.[2] The school committee of the town might attend to the same details for the town schools under their responsibility for "the general charge and superintendence."[3] But these duties have to do with the business aspect of school management, with school administration rather than with school supervision. By the year 1827, the two sets of powers had become sufficiently differentiated so that the functions of school supervision, those which have to do with the actual teaching activity, may be treated separately from those matters which are more directly fiscal and material. In this study, the powers of supervision as they came to be vested largely with the school committee are of particular concern.

Of the six powers connected with the supervision of class-

[1] *Revised Laws*, chap. xli., sec. 6.

[2] *Acts of 1827*, cxliii., sec. 6.

[3] *Ibid.*, cxliii., sec. 5.

room activity, not all were equally developed as distinct functions. Nor did they represent save in a crude way all the functions of supervision as they are known to-day under the conditions of expert supervision, as it is found in the large, progressive cities of our present time. In a modern educational system of to-day, the functions of supervision cluster about three factors in instruction. They are: (1) those which have reference to the teacher, (2) those which have reference to the course of study, and (3) those which have reference to the pupils. Of the six functions which were given to the school committees by the General Statutes of 1827, the first four—viz., appointment, certification, inspection, and supervision (in the narrower sense)—refer to the teacher. Assignment had not yet differentiated itself from appointment. The fifth function—the adoption of text-books—had reference to the course of study. The actual making of courses of study had not yet become a definite activity. The sixth function—the classification of pupils—had reference to the pupils directly. It was the vaguest of the functions implied by the legislation of 1827.

THE APPOINTMENT OF TEACHERS

Just when and how and through what agencies these powers or functions came into existence it will be interesting to note. As they seem to have appeared in the order mentioned, it will be well to consider them one at a time as they appeared. The first of these is the power to appoint teachers.

The simplicity of the earliest schools in the colonial period has already been suggested.[1] It consisted of some one to teach and some to be taught; and the only votes necessary for the establishment of a school in those days were two: (1) the vote providing funds for the payment of the teacher and (2) the vote selecting a teacher.[2] A special school structure was not regarded as a necessity at first. The school might meet at any convenient place.[3] So the appointment or election of the teacher was one of the earliest functions to come into existence. It dated from the very beginning of schools. In its antiquity it ranked with the provision for the support of schools. Sometimes

[1] See above, Chap. II., p. 10. [2] See above, Chap. II., p. 10 *et seq.*
[3] Martin, *Evol. Mass. Pub. School System*, pp. 51, 54, 77 *et seq.*

the first action toward the establishment of a school was the election of a teacher, sometimes it was the laying aside of funds for the payment of his recompense.[1]

At first the appointment of teachers was, generally speaking, exercised by the town meeting. This was particularly true in the third and fourth decades of the sixteenth century, though the practice was continued much later in certain instances. Among the towns which appointed the teacher through the town meeting were: Boston (1635),[2] Charlestown (1636),[3] Cambridge (1638),[4] Newbury (1639),[5] and Salem (1640).[6] The town of Dorchester, in 1645, laid down the regulation, that while the school wardens or overseers were to see that the town was provided with a schoolmaster, he was "not to be admitted into the place of Schoolemaster without the generall cōsent of the Inhabitants." [7]

There were a number of facts which tended to place the appointment of teachers in the hands of some authority other than that of the town meeting, which was an unwieldy body for attending to the details of government. It met only at intervals, and in the interim there were always details demanding attention. The town selectmen were necessary for affairs in general because of this fact. It is not surprising that the details of school management, along with other town business, came to be delegated. There were two facts in particular which had to do with the appointment of the teacher which influenced the delegation of that power to selectmen, special committees, or others. The first was the necessity of finding a teacher, if one was not available, so that the town would have some one to elect. The second was the necessity of coming to terms with such teacher when it was decided he was the proper person. Such details had to be attended to by some person or persons before the town could really vote upon the matter.

There is sufficient record to indicate that selectmen or special committees were authorized to find teachers which were to be approved by the town meeting. The above-mentioned regula-

[1] See above, Chap. II., pp. 8, 9 *et seq.*

[2] Boston, *Rep. Rec. Com.*, ii., 5.

[3] Barnard, *Amer. Jour. Educ.*, xxvii., 127.

[4] Cambridge, *Records*, p. 33.

[5] Coffin, *Hist. of Newbury*, p. 32.

[6] Felt, *Annals of Salem*, i., 427.

[7] Boston, *Rep. Rec. Com.*, iv., 54

tion laid down by the town of Dorchester is a distinct provision for such a method of getting a teacher. In 1649, it was "agreed that John Sherman Shall wright a letter: in the Townes name" to procure a certain teacher for the school at Watertown.[1] Dedham, in 1652, ordered its selectmen "to pcure a fitt schoole mr. at the begining of the sumer and if it pue difficult or not to be attayned: they may ppose the case to the Towne for further resolution." [2] In Plymouth, in 1692/3, the "Inhabitants of sd Towne voated that the Selectmen of sd towne shall Indeavour to get A scool master." [3] In 1691, the selectmen of Cambridge "Called Sir Hancock to keep scoole for the Town." [4] And the instances multiply in the records.

The instances where the town delegated town officials or other persons to agree with the teacher are even more numerous. A few typical instances will illustrate how the towns delegated the matter of contracting for the teacher's service. In 1650, the town meeting of Watertown chose Richard Norcross as teacher, and the selectmen proceeded to agree as to his payment.[5] In 1651, the town of Dorchester ordered that "the selectmen together with Mr Jones and Deacon wiswall should forthwith treate and agree with Mr henry Butler for to teach scoole." [6] Dedham, in 1661, records that two of its selectmen were "deputed to speack with Brother Metcalfe & treat with him about the Keepinge of the schoole." [7] In 1666, the Boston selectmen "Agreed with Mr Dannell Hinscheman" to assist the grammar school master. "Covenants made & concluded Betweene" the selectmen of Braintree and Mr. Thompson, the schoolmaster elect, were recorded in the year 1682/3.[8] In 1683, the town of Springfield authorized the selectmen to arrange the stipend of John Richards who had commenced to teach.[9] Other towns record similar delegations of function to selectmen or special committees.

From the selection of the teacher and agreeing with him regarding specific terms of payment, there was but a short step to actually choosing him without the express approbation of

[1] Watertown, *Records*, p. 18.

[2] Dedham, *Records*, i., 136.

[3] Plymouth, *Records*, i., 224.

[4] Cambridge, *Records*, p. 293.

[5] Watertown *Records*, pp. 21, 22.

[6] Boston, *Rep. Rec. Com.*, iv., 304.

[7] Dedham, *Records*, ii., 46.

[8] Boston, *Rep. Rec. Com.*, vii., 30

[9] Braintree, *Records*, p. 21.

the town meeting. Practically all of the above towns which deputed the power of finding, treating with, or agreeing with teachers, record subsequent votes which actually authorized some person or persons to provide, choose, hire, or appoint some person to teach school. This was the case with Dorchester in 1666, when the town voted that a committee of three "be desier and empowered to endeauor to p'cuer a Schol-Master." [1] In 1678, the selectmen of Watertown dismissed two teachers and hired another.[2] Springfield ordered its selectmen to "use their diligent care to provide a Schoolmaster" and to agree with him even if they were compelled to exceed the allotted amount of twenty pounds.[3] In May of 1700, Braintree ordered its selectmen to "be appointed & impowered a Committee to treeat & agree with Mr. Eells (or if he refuse some other) for a school master for the year ensueing." [4] Plymouth, in 1701, "Voted that A scoolmaster shall be hired for the yeare by the selectmen." [5] In 1703, the town of Boston "Voted that the Selectmen do take care to procure Some meet person to be an assistant to Mr. Ezekiell Chever." [6]

Thus the appointment of the teacher gradually passed out of the hands of the town meeting into the hands of the selectmen and special committees, more frequently into the hands of the former, particularly in the later part of the seventeenth century. In fact, the tendency of selectmen to care for the providing of teachers led to a recognition of the fact by the General Court. Up to the year 1692/3, the laws of the commonwealth had placed the responsibility for the maintenance of the teachers directly upon the towns.[7] With the statute of 1692/3, the responsibility was placed equally upon the town in general and the selectmen as its representatives. The law explicitly stated that "the selectmen and the inhabitants of such towns, respectively, shall take effectual care and make due provision for the settlement and maintenance of such school-master and masters." [8]

[1] Boston, *Rep. Rec. Com.*, iv., 136.
[2] Watertown, *Records*, p. 137.
[3] Springfield, *Records*, ii., 200.
[4] Braintree, *Records*, p. 47.
[5] Plymouth, *Records*, i., 289.
[6] Boston, *Rep. Rec. Com.*, viii., 28.
[7] None of the statutes of the General Court from 1647 to 1692/3 make mention of others than the town or township or the inhabitants thereof in stating the requirement for the maintenance of teachers.—*Records of Mass.*, ii., 203 *et seq.*
[8] *Prov. Acts & Res.*, i., 63.

Throughout the eighteenth century most of the towns entrusted the appointment of teachers to the selectmen, and, with more or less frequency, to special committees. This was particularly true in those communities which had no annual school committees for the provision of teachers and schooling. Even Boston, which had an annual committee for the inspection of schools, for the larger part of the century depended upon the selectmen for the selection of teachers, though the inspection or other special committees were sometimes given this privilege. The inspection committee existed in Boston after 1709/10 with considerable regularity, as has been shown.[1] There are many definite records after that date of appointments made by the selectmen. There are such records in 1711/2, 1718, 1726, 1728, 1729, and thereafter.[2]

Such towns as had no annual committees during the eighteenth century prior to the law of 1789 relied for the most part upon the selectmen. Specially appointed committees are found in use with greater frequency as the latter part of the century is reached. The town of Braintree makes little mention on its record of the appointment and dismissal of teachers. In 1708, 1715, and 1775, the selectmen seem to have attended to such matters.[3] In 1725 and 1728, special committees attended to the details of obtaining the teacher.[4] The Springfield selectmen were the main factors in providing masters in 1708, 1716, and 1717.[5] In 1730, Brookline appointed a committee of three to procure schoolmistresses.[6] After that time, in 1746, 1783, and 1787, the selectmen hired the teachers.[7] Plymouth, which tended strongly toward the use of committees, used the selectmen for the hiring of teachers in 1714. In 1722, 1723, 1724/5, and 1732, special committees were used.[8] Even such towns as Tisbury and Duxbury, which were moving toward the use of committees from the very start, note the selectmen as hiring or providing the teacher.[9]

[1] See above, Chap. VII., pp. 91–92.

[2] Boston, *Rep. Rec. Com.*, viii., 90, 136, 137, 204; xii., 4, 13; xvi., 284; xviii., 252; xxxi., 18.

[3] Braintree, *Records*, pp. 69, 86, 462.

[4] *Ibid.*, pp. 113, 217, 218.

[5] Springfield, *Records*, ii., 380, 400, 404.

[6] Brookline, *Records*, i., 136.

[7] *Ibid.*, i., 160, 325, 357, 362.

[8] Plymouth, *Records*, ii., 94, 217, 218, 220, 226, 232, 280, 281.

[9] Tisbury, *Records*, pp. 125, 129; Duxbury, *Records*, p. 242.

Such towns as developed the annual school committees for the providing of teachers early in the eighteenth century, having a special means for the appointment of teachers, did not utilize the selectmen or special committees. Such was the case among the towns Lunenburg, Fitchburg, Dudley, and Grafton.[1]

The appointment of teachers in the eighteenth century prior to the act of 1789 was largely in the hands of the selectmen. In many towns special committees were frequently used instead of the selectmen. In some towns where the annual committee had developed rapidly from the special temporary committees, the appointment of teachers was in the care of regularly elected school committees for that purpose.

With the act of 1789, there came an incidental recognition of the existing state of affairs, which in a sense legalized the methods employed. While the reading of the sections of the law concerning the maintenance of masters held the "town or district" responsible for the provision of grammar-school masters and elementary school teachers, it nevertheless sanctioned the delegation of such authority by the town or district to "Selectmen or Committee" of either temporary or standing type. In the section of the law which has to do with the certification and approval of instructors of youth who may be residents of the town in which the school is to be kept, a reference is made directly to "such Selectmen or Committee, who may be authorized to hire such schoolmaster." [2]

The act of 1789 stimulated both the district system and the movement for the appointment of regularly elected school committees.[3] The committees for the appointment of teachers had reflected the district organization to a greater or less extent from the very beginning, and after the law of 1789 the district committee on teachers was in evidence more than ever. The result was that, in the act of 1827, it was required, "That each town in this Commonwealth, which is or may be divided into school districts," shall choose a "prudential committee," consisting of one person who shall be "a resident in the district from which he shall be chosen," whose duty it shall be, beside caring for the material wants of the school, "to select and contract with a school teacher for his own district." [4]

[1] See above, Chapter VI., p. 76 *et seq.* [3] See above, Chap. VIII., p. 102 *et seq.*

[2] *Acts of 1789*, chap. xix., sec. 6. [4] *Acts of 1827*, chap. cxliii., sec. 6.

The law of 1827 specifically mentions only the hiring of district teachers by the district prudential committeemen. Neither in the law of 1826 or in that of 1827, where the town committee is treated at length, is there any mention of the specific duty of appointing teachers being given to the school committee, as is the case with certification, inspection, etc. It is altogether likely that the power to appoint teachers of town schools was assumed under the general power granted in the clause, "who shall have the general charge and superintendence of all the public schools in said town." [1]

Such an interpretation is borne out by the case of Boston. In 1790, the school committee was definitely authorized "to exercise all the Powers relating to the Schools & School Masters, which the Selectmen or such Committees are authorized by the Laws of this Commonwealth on the Votes of this Town to exercise." [2] Such an authorization was made each year thereafter.[3] When the town of Boston became the incorporated City of Boston in 1822, all these specifically mentioned duties, reiterated annually, were covered by the general clause, "the care and superintendence of the public schools." [4] The statement of this clause is not unlike the statement in the acts of 1826 and 1827, which was "the general charge and superintendence of all the public schools."

The inspection committee of Cambridge which, in 1770, had as one of its definite duties "to chuse a grammar schoolmaster for said town," [5] had its duties prescribed in the year 1795 by the following general authorization: the committee was "chosen for the purpose of superintending the schools in this town, and carrying into effect the School Act." [6]

The power of the appointment of teachers was exercised directly by the town meeting during the first few decades of colonial life. The selectmen, from about 1650 on, appointed the teachers with increasing frequency. In the later seventeenth century, special committees were sometimes used instead of the selectmen. In the eighteenth century, the selectmen still

[1] *Acts of 1826*, chap. clxx., sec. 1; *Acts of 1827*, chap. cxliii., sec. 5.

[2] Boston, *Rep. Rec. Com.*, xxxi., 219.

[3] *Ibid.*, xxxi., 245, 246, 284, 285 *et seq.*

[4] *Act of February 23, 1822*, sec. 19.

[5] Paige, *Hist. of Cambridge*, p. 375.

[6] *Ibid.*, p. 376.

tended to appoint the teacher. But special committees performed that power to an increasing extent. Certain towns began to appoint committees, whose regular business it was to procure teachers, particularly for the district schools. With the beginning of the nineteenth century, town and district committees were further differentiated, each appointing teachers for schools belonging to its own geographical unit. In 1827, the General Court definitely gave the power of appointing district school teachers to the district prudential committee. The acts of 1826 and 1827 gave such power in the case of town schools to the town school committee by giving it "general charge and superintendence" of the town schools.

CERTIFICATION

When the town elected a teacher, it was supposed to exercise some judgment as to whether or not the various persons that fell within their consideration were "fit and able to instruct." Some rough standard for the approval of teachers was implied in the very act of electing teachers, long before certification was recognized as a distinct function. Hence the power of certification in the earliest period may be regarded as being undifferentiated from the appointment of teachers.

Indeed, some standard of fitness as to the proper persons to be chosen as schoolmasters was laid down by the earliest laws of the General Court upon the subject of schools. The earliest law of the commonwealth, the law of 1647, implied such a standard of fitness. In the matter of teachers for the secondary or grammar schools, it was expressly stated to the towns that "they shall set up a gramer schoole, ye master thereof being able to instruct youth so farr as they may be fited for ye university." In referring to the elementary school, it was stated that every township "shall then forthwth appoint one wthin their towne to teach all such children as shall resort to him to write & reade." [1] These references were as much descriptions of the schools and their courses of study as anything else, but they laid down a standard for the fitness of teachers at the same time.

In this earlier period, when there was no definite and clear

[1] *Records of Mass.*, ii., 203.

function of certification set forth by the laws, a standard of fitness was nevertheless implied. So the town of Dorchester, in 1645, imposed the duty upon its school wardens of supplying an "able and sufficient Schoolemaster." [1] Dedham, in 1652, voted that its selectmen "shall attend to pcure a fitt schoole mr." [2] In other instances the town itself set up standards in addition to those of the colonial law in asking that a master be provided. Dorchester, in 1639, wanted "such a schoolemaster as shall undertake to teach english latin and other tongues and also writing." [3] In 1650, Watertown hired a teacher to instruct "Children to Reed & write & soe much of Lattin, according to an Order of Courtt," and in addition to teach maids to write and "such as desire to Cast acompt." [4] In 1652/3, Dedham specifically agreed to pay Jacob Farrow a certain amount if "he undertakes to teach to read English & the Accidence & to write & the Knowledg & art of Arithmeticke & the rules & practice thereof." [5]

Certification first appeared as a definite function when the General Court passed an act in 1654, commending "it to the serious consideration & speciall care of the ouseers of the colledge, & the selectmen in the seuerall townes, not to admitt or suffer any such to be contynued in the office or place of teaching, educating, or instructing of youth or child, in the colledge or schooles, that haue manifested ymselves vnsound in the fayth, or scandelous in theire liues, & not giueing due satisfaction according to the rules of Christ." [6]

From this act of 1654 until 1701/2, when there was further legislation upon this subject, there were further references to a "meete" man for a teacher. Subsequent acts of the General Court made use of similar phrases. In 1683, the law of the General Court referring to grammar and writing schools, stated that the masters "shall be fit and able to instruct youth as said law directs." [7] The act of 1692/3 specifically demanded that the grammar school masters should be "some discreet person of good conversation, well instructed in the tongues." [8] Plymouth colony, which in this period was separate from Massachusetts

[1] Boston, *Rep. Rec. Com.*, iv., 54.
[2] Dedham, *Records*, i., 136.
[3] Boston, *Rep. Rec. Com.*, iv., 39.
[4] Watertown, *Records*, p. 21.
[5] Dedham, *Records*, i., 213.
[6] *Rec. of Mass.*, iii., 343, 344.
[7] *Ibid.*, v., 414, 415.
[8] *Prov. Acts & Res.*, i., 63.

Bay, enacted a law ordering schools for which "any meet man shalbe obtained." [1]

It is not clear just how far the selectmen of the various towns exercised the duty commended to them by the colonial government. The selectmen of the town of Boston, at least, seemed to attend to the matter. In 1666, the selectmen of this community sent for one of those who was keeping school in the town and he was "forbideng to keepe schoole any longer." [2] The following year the selectmen voted that "Mr Will Howard hath liberty to keep a wrighting schoole, to teach childeren to writte and to keep accounts." [3] The town of Dorchester, in 1667/8, instructed its special committee "to agree with such a man as they shall Judge meete." [4]

The General Court was evidently not satisfied with the type of teacher that was being maintained in the schools, the grammar schools particularly. So in the year 1701/2 the power of certificating grammar-school masters was taken from the selectmen and given to the ministers. The law is as follows:

> Every grammar-school master [is] to be approved by the minister of the town, and the ministers of the two next adjacent towns, or any two of them, by certificate under their hands. [5]

This law was reaffirmed ten years later, in 1711/2. [6]

In the same act, owing to the fact that ministers were serving as schoolmasters, largely to meet the requirements of the letter of the law, [7] a special disability was placed upon established ministers of towns. They could not be certificated to teach in the town grammar school. The law provided "that no minister of any town be deemed, held or accepted to be the school master of such town within the intent of the law." [8] This disability was repeated in the school act of 1789, [9] and was not removed until the year 1811. [10]

The origin of the law requiring certification by the ministers is somewhat interesting. The precedent for it seems to have existed in the admission of persons to the place of freemen in

[1] *Plymouth, Col. Records*, xi., 247.
[2] Boston, *Rep. Rec. Com.*, vii., 32, 33.
[3] *Ibid.*, vii., 36.
[4] *Ibid.*, iv., 145.
[5] *Prov. Acts & Res.*, i., 470.
[6] *Ibid.*, i., 681, 682.
[7] Martin, *Evol. Mass. Pub. School System*, p. 71.
[8] *Prov. Acts & Res.*, i., 470.
[9] *Acts of 1789*, chap. xix., sec. 6.
[10] *Act of Feb. 26, 1811.*

the towns. There was, in the edition of the laws for 1649, a provision that "no man shall be admitted to the freedome of this Common-wealth, but such as are members of some of the Churches, within the limits of this Iurisduction."[1] With such a religious test, it was most natural that the ministers should sooner or later come to issue the certificate of such membership. This is exactly what occurred. In 1664, the General Court among other things ordered "That from henceforth all English men presenting a Certificate under the hand of the Ministers, or Minister of the Place where they dwell, that they are Orthodox in Religion, and not Vicious in their Lives," should be admitted. The selectmen were required to certify likewise that the person was a freeholder and "Rateable to the Country."[2] Here, then, was the precedent for the certification act of 1701/2. The ministers were to certify in the case of freemen, "that they are Orthodox in Religion, and not Vicious in their Lives." They were, therefore, the proper persons to certify that grammar school masters had not "manifested ymselves vnsound in the fayth, or scandelous in theire liues."[3]

That the ministers actually did attend to the matter of certification in at least one town, is indicated by a chance bit of evidence in the records. In 1724/5, there was inserted in the records of the town meetings of Plymouth a certificate of approbation signed by three ministers.[4] The certificate reads as follows:

Wee the Subscribers Ministers of the Gospell do hereby signify that we do aprobate Mr John Sparhawk as a person well Capasitated and qualified to teach a Grammer School & accordingly do recommend him to the Town of Plymouth or any other Town where God in his providence shall see Cause to Call him

Dated at Plymouth
this 21st day of
January 1724/5

BENJAMIN ALLEN
NATHANIEL LEONARD
JOSEPH STACEY

Ten years after the passage of the act requiring definite certification of grammar-school masters by the ministers, a similar

[1] Whitmore, *Col. Laws*, i., 153.

[2] *Ibid.*, i., 3.

[3] This was the language of the act of 1654 which was the first certification law of the General Court.—*Rec. of Mass.*, iii., 343, 344.

[4] *Plymouth Col. Records*, ii., 229–230.

act required elementary teachers to be certificated by the selectmen. The law reads as follows:

> That no person or persons shall or may presume to set up or keep a school for the teaching and instructing of children or youth in reading, writing, or any other science, but such as are of sober and good conversation, and have the allowance and approbation of the selectmen of the town in which any such school is to be kept; grammar-school masters to have approbation as the law in such case already provides.[1]

A fine of forty shillings was imposed as a penalty for the violation of this law, the same to be for the benefit of the poor of the town.

Incidental mention of this law occurs more frequently than in the case of the law regarding grammar-school masters. Possibly this was because of the more frequent need to approve elementary school teachers. There were more of them. The town of Boston, in 1735, forbade the keeping of a school by an unapproved woman.[2] Wenham has two records of approbation of teachers by the selectmen. In 1743, the selectmen, "being well satisfied of his ability for that service, and his sober and good conversation, do approbate said Jonathan Perkins."[3] In 1746, it was Mrs. Elizabeth Kimball who was "approved of and approbated to keep school."[4] In the town archives of Oxford, there is filed a certificate of an elementary teacher.[5] It is as follows:

> OXFORD, Dec. 19th, 1769.
>
> Whereas the Sqardron att the South Part of Oxford have Chosen Mr. Samuel Harris to be their Schoolmaster for their term of Schooling we the Subscribers approve of him for a Schoolmaster and Recommend him to be qualfyed as the Law directs for a Reading and Writing.
>
> EDWARD DAVIS,
> HEZA. STONE,
> EPH'M BALLARD,
> WILLIAM WATSON,
> Select Men of Oxford.

In 1784, a committee appointed by the town of Boston to consider school affairs, "specially recommended to the Select-

[1] *Prov. Acts & Res.*, i., 681, 682.
[2] Boston, *Rep. Rec. Com.*, xiii., 274.
[3] Allen, *Hist. of Wenham*, pp. 112, 113.
[4] *Ibid.*, p. 113.
[5] Daniels, *Hist. of Oxford*, p. 773.

men to take Care that no Person may be Allowed to Open a Private School without their Approbation agreeable to a good and Salutary Law of the Commonwealth." [1] The town went further than the law when at this same meeting it was "Voted, that the Selectmen be directed not to approve of or continue any Person as a Private Schoolmaster within the Town unless such Master shall agree to be governed by such regulations as to the Prise of his Instruction as the Selectmen from time to time see fit to make." [2] The interesting facts brought out here are that the law applied to private masters as well as to those in the public schools, and that the town could and did go beyond the standard laid down by the law of the General Court.

No further changes were made in the certification laws until the year 1789, when a highly complicated law upon the whole subject of certification was passed by the General Court. In general, the power to certificate all types of teachers was placed in the hands of the ministers and the selectmen or school committee of the town. The law practically required two certificates before certification was complete, one from the minister or ministers, and one from the selectmen or the school committee of the town.[3]

The subject is dealt with in two different portions of the law. The first part had reference to "the President, Professors and Tutors of the University at Cambridge, Preceptors and Teachers of Academies and all other instructors of youth." The first certificate required was one of academic proficiency. It could be one of two kinds: (1) it could be "satisfactory evidence" that the candidate had "received an education at some College or University," or (2) "a certificate from a learned minister, well skilled in the Greek and Latin languages, settled in the town or place where the school is proposed to be kept, or two other such ministers in the vicinity thereof." If the certificate was "for a Grammar School," it had to state expressly, "that he is of competent skill in the Greek and Latin languages for the said purpose." The second certificate required was one of moral character. It could come from one of three sources: (1) from the "settled minister" of the place where the candidate lived, (2) from the selectmen of such place, or (3) from the

[1] Boston, *Rep. Rec. Com.*, xxxi., 17.
[2] *Ibid*, xxxi., 18.
[3] *Acts of 1789*, chap. xix., secs. 4, 5, 6, 9.

school committee of said town. This second certificate might be waived if the person resided in the town where the school was to be kept, but the selectmen or committee were "specially to attend to his morals," which amounted to the same thing substantially.[1]

The second part of the law had reference to the master or mistress of "schools for the education of children in the most early stages of life." Two certificates were required in this case as well, but they were not differentiated as to the facts certified, but as to the persons certifying. Both certificates must state "that he or she is a person of sober life and conversation, and well qualified to keep such school." One was to come from the selectmen or the school committee of such town. The other was to come from "a learned minister settled therein, if such there be." The phrase, "if such there be," suggests that the second certificate might not always be necessary.[2]

This law excluded another class than the ministers from eligibility to certification. It provided "That no person shall be permitted to keep within this Commonwealth, any school described in this act, unless in consequence of an act of naturalization, or otherwise, he shall be a citizen of this or some other of the United States." A penalty of twenty pounds per month was imposed for violation of this section of the law.[3]

In 1824, the certification of elementary teachers was to be accomplished exactly as that of grammar-school masters in the act of 1789. Towns with less than five thousand inhabitants were permitted to substitute for masters "well instructed in the Latin & Greek languages," teachers "well qualified to instruct youth in Orthography, Reading, writing, Arithmetic, English Grammar, Geography and good behavior." The manner of certification remained as it had been in the case of the Latin and Greek masters.[4] This was a larger and more definite requirement than for elementary teachers.

In 1826, the matter of the agency of certification of the various types of teachers was greatly simplified. The whole matter was placed in the hands of the town school committee, who could "require full and satisfactory evidence of the good character and qualifications of said instructors, conformably to the

[1] *Acts of 1789*, chap. xix., secs. 5, 6.
[2] *Ibid.*, chap xix., secs. 9, 10.
[3] *Ibid.*, chap. xix., sec. 11
[4] *Act of Feb. 18, 1824.*

laws now in force." Teachers were to receive no compensation for service until the law had been complied with.[1]

The act of 1827 left the agency for certificating teachers exactly where it was. It gave the right of "personal examination" to the school committee in determining the qualifications of candidates. The classes of certificated teachers were changed. No mention is made of "Professors and Tutors of the University at Cambridge," or of the "preceptors and Teachers of Academies." Reference is made solely to the classes of teachers corresponding to the types of school required of various communities by the commonwealth. These were all to be certificated by the same agency, the school committee.[2] The requirements for certification covered a different range of subjects. The first class was to be able to instruct children in orthography, writing, English grammar, geography, arithmetic, and good behavior. The second class, in addition to the subjects of the first class, was to be competent to instruct in the history of the United States, book-keeping by single entry, geometry, surveying, and algebra. The third class, in addition to the subjects of both the preceding classes, was to be able to instruct in the Latin and Greek languages, history, rhetoric, and logic.[3]

The certification of teachers has evolved along three general lines : (1) in the agencies used for certification; (2) in the classes of teachers certificated; and (3) in the standard set for teaching certificates. Certification seems not to have appeared as a function, distinct from appointment, until the law of 1654 was passed, when the matter of the qualifications of the university instructors was placed in the hands of the overseers, and that of other teachers in the hands of the town selectmen. In 1701/2 the certification of grammar-school teachers was given to the ministers. In 1711/2, the selectmen were required to certificate elementary teachers. In the law of 1789, all three types of teachers—college, grammar-school, and elementary school—were considered. The power to certificate them lay jointly with the ministers and selectmen or school committee. With the laws of 1826 and 1827, the whole matter was placed in the hands of the school committee, where it rests to-day.[4]

Up to the law of 1827, college instructors as well as private

[1] *Acts of 1826*, chap. clxx., sec. 1.
[2] *Ibid.*, chap. cxliii., sec. 5.
[3] *Ibid.*, chap. cxliii., sec. 1.
[4] *Revised Laws*, chap. xlii., sec. 28.

school teachers seemed to have come under the certification law. With this law, only the qualifications of teachers in the three classes of public schools required of communities by the state are described. For a period of about a hundred and ten years, settled ministers were not allowed to teach the grammar-school; and after 1789 none but citizens of the United States could be certificated.

In the beginning, the moral and religious requirement was urged as the factor demanding most attention. It gradually became subordinate as a matter requiring particular attention, and the academic requirement received the most detailed treatment. The period of greatest development in this respect was the early nineteenth century. The rapidity with which the academic standard for certification rose may be well illustrated by the case of the grammar-school master. In 1789, he had to be certified in two subjects, Latin and Greek. In 1827, he had to be certified in sixteen subjects.

VISITATION AND INSPECTION

The function of the visitation and inspection of schools is, logically as well as historically, supplementary to the function of certification. Certification is a method of protection designed to keep immoral and inefficient teachers out of the school. Inspection is a method designed to keep such from continuing in the schoolroom, once they have been certificated and employed. At first, inspection was intended largely for the patrons of the school. It was a method by which they could inform themselves, through their official representatives, as to the methods of discipline and instruction pursued. Not until later did it come to be the foundation for the direction and supervision of the teacher's work.

It has been said that the ministers were the early inspectors of the schools, particularly the Latin schools.[1] A study of the first established inspection committees seems to corroborate such

[1] Dr. Brown, in his *Making of our Middle Schools*, says: "In the New England towns it seems to have been taken as a matter of course that the schools should be inspected by the ministers (p. 149). Mr. Martin, in his work on the *Evolution of the Massachusetts Public School System*, says that the "Latin schools were under the constant and vigilant supervision of the ministers" (p. 64).

statement in two ways. The first committees of inspection were committees for some particular grammar-school. These first committees generally included ministers as *ex-officio* members.[1] In fact, in writing their report to the town, the special committee which recommended the appointment of the first school inspectors for the Latin school of the town of Boston definitely referred to some more or less distinct precedent. No officially constituted inspectors, prior to this Boston committee of 1709/10, are a matter of known record, and it is possible that the reference was to the practice of the ministers visiting the Latin school as part of their pastoral duties to the community. This report creating inspectors was made after consultation with the ministers of the town, and they may possibly have informed the committee of their practice.[2] The protest of Mr. Mather, one of the ministers, against the use of laymen in visitation would corroborate the statement.[3] Finally, the earlier arrangements of the sub-committees so as always to include ministers on those committees which visited the Latin grammar schools, suggests that the momentum of tradition was at work.[4] It is altogether probable that the ministers visited at least the grammar-school in the period prior to the first official organization of school visitors by the town.

There was no recognition of the function of visitation under any general school statute of the General Court. The function gets its first official recognition from the town government. The General Court did, however, in a special act regulating the grammar-school at Ipswich in 1755/6, give the joint committee of selectmen and surviving feoffees the right "to inspect said school and schoolmaster."[5] The early history of school inspection is connected primarily with the schools of special towns, and of Boston in particular.

While there was this school committee having the power to inspect at Ipswich, in 1755/6; a committee appointed by the town of Cambridge for its grammar school in 1744 and 1770[6];

1 *Cf.* above, Chap. VII.
2 Boston, *Rep. Rec. Com.*, viii., 65.
3 Martin, *Evol. Mass. Pub. School System*, p. 65.
4 Boston, *Rep. Rec. Com.*, xiii., 134.
5 *Prov. Acts & Res.*, iii., 891–893.
6 Paige, *Hist. of Cambridge*, p. 375.

and one to be chosen by the town and the squadron at Lancaster for a squadron Latin school in 1788,[1] the history of the movement for inspection during the colonial period is really the history of the inspection committees of Boston, for there the idea started and developed through many stages.

The development in Boston was along two conspicuous lines. First, the officially denominated membership of the inspecting committee changed. Second, there was a broadening of the scope of visitation. The membership was differently constituted during three different periods: (1) in 1710 and 1711, the ministers and five learned gentlemen constituted the committee; (2) from 1714 to 1718 inclusive, the ministers and selectmen were officially named; (3) from 1721 to 1789, the selectmen and others invited by them, among whom were always some ministers, were the official school inspectors. The scope of the annual committees for inspection, as to the number and types of schools visited, differed with each of the above-mentioned periods. In the first period, the committeemen were visitors of a particular Latin grammar-school, as in the case of Ipswich, Cambridge, and Lancaster. In the second period, the committee visited a class of schools—all grammar-schools of the town, of which there were then two. In the third period, the committee of inspection visited all the schools supported by the town, writing schools as well as grammar-schools.[2]

With the school act of the year 1789, the state gave its first general recognition to the function of school visitation and inspection. In that year it required that all town and district schools be visited and inspected, and committed such obligation to a joint committee of the ministers and selectmen or school committee. The law reads as follows:

> And it shall be the duty of the minister or ministers of the gospel and the Selectmen (or such other persons as shall be specially chosen by each town or district for that purpose,) of the several towns or districts . . . once in every six months at least, and as much oftener as they shall determine it necessary, to visit and inspect the several schools in their respective towns and districts, and shall inquire into the regulation and discipline thereof, and the proficiency of the scholars therein, giving reasonable notice of the time of their visitation.[3]

---

[1] Marvin, *Hist. of Lancaster*, pp. 349, 350.

[2] See above, Chap. VII.

[3] *Acts of 1789*, chap. xix., sec. 8.

Under this act the committee on inspection could have been a committee of the "town or district." But the fact that the inspection committees had usually been town committees, coupled with the fact that the selectmen who were to be used if there were no existing school committee, were distinctly town rather than district officers, seemed to have made most of the committees, appointed especially for visitation and inspection, town committees. In consequence, when the town committee was required by state law in 1826, it was given the function of school inspection.[1]

The law of 1826 not only changed the agency of school inspection from a joint committee of ministers and selectmen (or special school committee) to a town committee with a membership which was not at all *ex-officio,* but it changed certain details of the method of supervision, which are important. In the first place, visitation was made a more frequent matter. Before, the committee on inspection was required to visit schools once in six months. Now, in the case of district schools, two visits were required of the whole committee each year; but they had to be made at a specified time. Town schools had to be visited each quarter instead of each half-year. Finally, some "one or more of said committee" had to visit all the schools at least once a month. Where before "reasonable notice of the time of their visitation" had to be given the teacher, it was expressly stated by the new law that visits were to be made "without giving previous notice thereof to the instructors." The permission given to the committee to delegate its more frequent visitations to some person or persons who might visit whenever he chose without notice is significant. In a sense it marks one aspect of the beginning of the movement which led to the rise of the school superintendent.

The portion of the act of 1826, which includes the treatment of the subject of school inspection, is as follows:

It shall be the duty of said committee, to visit the schools in said town, which are kept through the year, at least once a quarter, for the purpose of making a careful examination of the same, and to see that the scholars are properly supplied with books; also, to inquire into the regulation and discipline of such schools, and the proficiency of the scholars therein; and it shall also be the duty of said committee to visit each of

[1] *Acts of 1826*, chap. clxx., sec. 1.

the district schools in said town, for the purposes aforesaid, on some day during the first week of the commencement thereof, and also on some day during the last two weeks of the same; and it shall further be the duty of one or more of said committee to visit all the schools in the town, at least once a month, for the purposes aforementioned, without giving previous notice thereof to the instructors. . . .[1]

The act of the following year made no changes in the method of inspecting schools, save in one important particular. The law of the year 1826 allowed the town committee for "the general charge and superintendence of all the public schools" to delegate to "one or more" of its number the monthly or more frequent visitation of the schools. The law of 1827 increased this privilege, so that even the two stated visits to the district schools at the beginning and close of school could be made by some one or more of the committee. The whole committee was now required to make only the quarterly visits to such schools as were town schools.[2]

The inspection of the teacher's work was a function which appeared later than certification. The scope of its application was less wide. It was not applied to college instructors or to private school teachers, as was certification. It was a power which grew up primarily in connection with the public schools. It had its beginning, so far as can be determined, in the visitation of the town Latin schools by the ministers. When this function was recognized by the town government, the ministers were usually made a joint committee with the selectmen or other freemen to perform the duty of visitation. It was through these same agencies that the state first required the general exercise of the function. Finally, the state placed it in the hands of the town committee, where it remained.

DIRECTION AND SUPERVISION

In a sense, any exercise of deliberate control over the teacher and his work in the classroom, may be termed "supervision" in the broad sense. It matters little whether the control is exercised upon the basis of the teacher's previous training in

[1] *Acts of 1826*, chap. clxx., sec. 1.

[2] *Acts of 1827*, chap. cxliii., sec. 5. One minor change was made. The beginning visit to the district school could be made any time during the first two weeks instead of during the first week.

certification, upon his personal qualifications in appointment, or upon the kind of text-books used. It is in each case supervision of the educational activity in a more or less direct way. But the term "supervision" is also used in a more restricted sense, in the sense of actual direction of the teacher, in his methods of teaching and discipline.

By the time that the school committees were made general agencies of school control in 1827, the function of directing or supervising the teacher's methods of work had appeared as one of the powers of the town school committee. It was one further step beyond certification and inspection. It has been suggested that as certification was designed to keep inefficient teachers from being employed, inspection was designed to keep the inefficient teacher from continuing to be employed. There were two ways that inspection could be the basis for accomplishing this desired end. If a teacher's work was discovered to be weak upon inspection, the school authority could (1) discharge or decline to rehire such teacher, or (2) so direct and supervise his work so that it would become more effective. The latter alternative is what we understand by supervision of the teacher in the restricted sense.

The use of inspection as a basis for these two attitudes towards the teacher, dismissal and direction, may be illustrated by two instances from the records of the town of Boston. In 1722, the visiting committee of selectmen and gentlemen reported to the town that they had visited one of the writing masters, and "are of Opinion That it will be no Service to the Town to Continue, mr Anger in that Employ." Mr. Anger was discharged.[1] In 1753, the selectmen were requested to visit the schools more often and were instructed to "give such Directions to the Masters of Said Schools" concerning their government and egulation, "as they shall judge needful."[2] When inspection was used to gain knowledge for the direction of the teacher's work along more effective lines, the function of supervision appeared.

This direction of the teacher's work, in connection with the visitation and inspection of schools, appeared as a definite duty and power of the visiting committee of Boston with the above

[1] Boston, *Rep. Rec. Com.*, viii., 164, 165.

[2] *Ibid.*, xiv., 233.

order of the year 1753. But the function had really had a precedent in an earlier action of the town. In 1709/10, when the committee of inspection was first established, one of the functions of the inspectors was "to consult and Advise of further Methods for ye Advancement of Learning and the Good Government of the Schoole." [1] With the very inception of the idea of school inspection there was some notion that the visitation was to be used for some direction of the teacher. But the power of the committee was purely advisory. They had no authority to direct the teacher. They could merely "consult and Advise." Not till 1753 was the inspection committee given actual power to direct and supervise the teacher's activity. The regulations for the visiting committee in 1789 definitely reiterated this grant of power to the inspection committee, "whose business it shall be to . . . give such advice to the Masters as they shall think proper." [2] In 1822, when Boston became a city, this power was included with other supervisory powers under the general terms, "the care and superintendence of the public schools." [3]

There were other towns which, during this same period, seemed to recognize the direction of the teacher's work as a special function. In 1776, the town of Fitchburg did "impower the Schools Committee to Give orders to such Master or Masters as they shall imploy in said Service." [4] In 1797, the Tisbury district committees were "to provide masters for each destrict and to Superintend the Same." [5] In 1795, a Cambridge committee was "chosen for the purpose of superintending the schools." [6] Just what the terms "Superintend" and "Superintending" signify, is not perfectly clear, as in the case of Boston.

The first apparent recognition of the function of direction and supervision of the teacher's work by the state law was in 1826, when a general phrase, such as that which was used in describing the powers of the Boston Committee in 1822, was used. The law of 1826 provided for a committee in each town which was to "have the general charge and superintendence of all the public schools." [7] The phrase was repeated in the law

[1] Boston, *Rep. Rec. Com.*, viii., 65.
[2] *Ibid.*, xxxi., 209.
[3] *Act of Feb. 23, 1822*, sec. 19.
[4] Fitchburg, *Records*, i., 133.
[5] Tisbury, *Records*, p. 305.
[6] Paige, *Hist. of Cambridge*, p. 376.
[7] *Acts of 1826*, chap. clxx., sec. 1.

of 1827.[1] Such general terms are used to-day as an inclusive term for the various supervisory functions. The same identical phrase is used to denote the powers of the school committee.[2] The duty of the modern school superintendent of a Massachusetts town is still given in a similar manner. He is one, "who, under the direction and control of the committee, shall have the care and supervision of the public schools." [3]

The power to direct and supervise the teacher's activity in the classroom has appeared as a power in connection with the rise of committees of inspection. In fact, it is a function which is largely dependent upon the functions of visitation and inspection, which, in a sense, constitutes its basis. It is a function that has been associated with the committee idea from the very beginning. There is not much evidence to show that it was regarded with any such importance as it was in a later period.

ADOPTION OF TEXT-BOOKS

There is little to be said about the other two important powers possessed by the school committees of the year 1827. The power of prescribing text-books was first given to the town committee in 1826, when the following was passed as part of the law:

> Be it further enacted, That the school committee of each town shall direct and determine the classbooks to be used in the respective classes, in the public district and town schools of the town.

The committee was permitted to buy a supply of books to be sold at cost to the pupils at some specified place.[4] The following year the power of the committee to change books then in use was restricted, as follows:

> Provided, nevertheless, that in cases where children are already provided with books, which shall not be considered by the committee as being extremely faulty, in comparison with others which might be obtained and which may be possessed in such numbers as to admit of the proper and convenient classification of the school, then, and in that case, the committee shall not direct the purchase of new books, without first obtaining the consent of the parents, masters, or guardians of a majority of the children, so already provided for, under the term of two years from

---

[1] *Acts of 1827*, chap. cxliii., sec. 5.

[2] *Revised Laws*, chap. xlii., sec. 27.

[3] *Ibid.*, chap. xlii., sec. 40.

[4] *Acts of 1826*, chap. clxx., sec. 2.

the passing of this act, unless books become so worn as to be unfit for use: Provided, also, that said committee shall never direct any school books to be purchased or used, in any of the schools under their superintendence, which are calculated to favour any particular religious sect or tenet.[1]

CLASSIFICATION OF PUPILS

The power to classify pupils was present only to a very slight degree. It was expressly given to the town school committee to classify the children as between the lower and the higher schools. The law of 1827 states that it shall "be the duty of said committee to determine the number and qualifications of the scholars, to be admitted into the school kept for the use of the whole town."[2] This power to say what children should go to the grammar-school had been placed in the hands of the selectmen by the act of 1789.[3] "Proper and convenient classification of the school" was made a determining factor in the matter of adopting text-books, by the act of 1827,[4] and it is probable that this matter was one of the powers implied under the general term "care and superintendence," as it is not specifically mentioned elsewhere. To what extent this power was exercised is not known.

After almost two centuries there had been evolved a specialized instrument for the control and supervision of the public schools—the school committee. With the year 1827, the state had required the utilization of school committees in two forms. Every town was required to maintain a committee for the general charge and superintendence of the schools. Where a town was divided into school districts, a district prudential committee of one was required for each subdivision. These were the two agencies for managing school affairs. In these same two centuries there had been evolved six important powers of school supervision, some more fully developed than others. Five of these six powers rested within the authority of the town school committee in the year 1827. Certification, inspection, supervision, the prescription of text books, and the classification of pupils, to the extent that they existed, were duties and powers of the town committee. The appointment of teachers, for the district schools, where such existed, was definitely delegated to the

[1] *Acts of 1827*, chap. cxliii., sec. 7.
[2] *Ibid.*, chap. cxliii., sec. 5.
[3] *Ibid.*, chap. xix., sec. 3.
[4] *Ibid.*, chap. cxliii., sec. 7.

district prudential committees. It is probable that the appointment of teachers for the advanced town schools and for the elementary school, where the town was not districted, was a duty of the town school committee. Thus, with the growing complexity of school affairs, there had arisen specialized agencies of control and supervision, with the power to exercise certain more or less well-differentiated functions of school supervision.

BIBLIOGRAPHY OF WORKS CONSULTED

TOWN RECORDS

(*Arranged alphabetically by towns*)

Boston. Reports of the record commissioners of the City of Boston. 32 vols. Boston, 1881–1903.

Braintree. Records of the town of Braintree. 1640 to 1793. Randolph, Mass., 1886.

Brookline. Muddy River and Brookline records, 1634–1838. By the inhabitants of Brookline in town meeting. Vol. I. Brookline, 1875.

Cambridge. The records of the town of Cambridge (formerly Newtowne), Mass. 1630–1703. The records of the town meetings, and of the selectmen. . . . Vol. II. Cambridge, 1901.

Dedham. Early records of Dedham (Mass.), 1636–1673, with the selectmen's day book. 2 vols. Dedham, 1892–1894.

Dorchester. Fourth report of the record commissioners of the City of Boston. Boston, 1880.

Dudley. Town records of Dudley, Massachusetts, 1732–1754. 2 vols. Pawtucket, R. I., 1893–1894.

Duxbury. Copy of the old records of the town of Duxbury, Mass., from 1642 to 1770. Plymouth, 1893.

Fitchburg. The old records of the town of Fitchburg, Mass. 1764–1844. 6 vols. Fitchburg, 1898–1903.

Groton. The early records of Groton, Mass. 1662–1707. Groton, 1880.

Lancaster. The early records of Lancaster, Mass. 1643–1725. Lancaster, 1884.

Lunenburg. The early records of the town of Lunenburg, Mass., including that part which is now Fitchburg. 1719–1764. Fitchburg, 1896.

Oxford. The records of Oxford . . . from the earliest date, 1630 . . . Albany, 1894.

Plymouth. Records of the town of Plymouth. 1636–1743. 2 vols. Plymouth, 1889–1892.

Springfield. The first century of the history of Springfield. The official records from 1636 to 1736. . . . 2 vols. Springfield, 1898–1899.

Tisbury. Records of the town of Tisbury, Mass., beginning June 29, 1669, and ending May 16, 1864. Boston, 1903.

Watertown. Watertown records comprising the first and second books of town proceedings. . . . Watertown, 1894.

Weston. Records of the first precinct, 1746–1754, and of the town, 1754–1803. Boston, 1893.

Weston. Records of the town clerk. 1804–1826. Boston, 1894.

RECORDS AND LAWS OF THE COLONIES AND STATE

(*Arranged chronologically by periods treated*)

Shurtleff, Nathaniel B. (editor). Records of the governor and company of the Massachusetts Bay in New England. 1628–1686. 5 vols. Boston, 1853–1854.

Whitmore, William H. A bibliographical sketch of the laws of the Massachusetts colony from 1630 to 1686, in which are included the Body of Liberties of 1641, and the records of the Court of Assistants, 1641-1644. Boston, 1890.

Whitmore, William H. (editor). The colonial laws of Massachusetts. Reprinted from the edition of 1660, with the supplements to 1672, containing also the Body of Liberties of 1641. Boston, 1889.

Whitmore, William H. (editor). The colonial laws of Massachusetts. Reprinted from the edition of 1672, with the supplements through 1686. Boston, 1887.

Shurtleff, Nathaniel B. (editor). Records of the colony of New Plymouth in New England. 1633–1692. 12 vols. Boston, 1855–1861.

Ames, Ellis, and **Goodell, Abner Cheney** (editors). The acts and resolves, public and private, of the Province of the Massachusetts Bay: to which are prefixed the charters of the province. . . . 1692–1780. 8 vols. Boston, 1869–1896.

Massachusetts. The perpetual laws of the commonwealth of Mass., from the establishment of its Constitution in the year 1780, to the end of the year 1800 . . . in 3 vols. Boston, 1801.

Massachusetts. The laws of the commonwealth of Massachusetts, passed from the year 1780, to the end of the year 1800. . . . 2 vols. Boston, 1801.

Massachusetts. The laws of the commonwealth of Massachusetts, from Nov. 28, 1780, to February 28, 1807. . . . 3 vols. Boston, 1807.

Massachusetts. The public and general laws of the commonwealth of Massachusetts, from February 28, 1807, to February 16, 1816.

Massachusetts. Acts and resolves of the commonwealth of Massachusetts passed by the General Court, 1819–1827. Boston, 1819–1827.

Massachusetts. The revised laws of the commonwealth of Massachusetts relating to public instruction. Enacted by the legislature Nov. 21, 1901, to take effect Jan. 1, 1902, with amendments and additions to June, 1904. Boston, 1904.

HISTORIES OF PARTICULAR SCHOOLS.

(*Arranged alphabetically by towns*)

Boston. Catalogue of the Boston Public Latin School, established in 1635. With an historical sketch prepared by Henry F. Jenks. Boston, 1886.

Charlestown. Free school in Charlestown. Barnard, Amer. Jour. of Educ., xxvii., 127.

Dorchester. The free town school of Dorchester. Barnard, Amer. Jour. of Educ., xvi., 105.

Hadley. The Hopkins Foundation—The Hopkins School at Hadley. Barnard, Amer. Jour. of Educ., xxvii., 145.

Ipswich. Hammatt, Abraham. Address, delivered on the two hundredth anniversary of the foundation of the grammar school at Ipswich. Antiquarian Papers, Ipswich. Vol. i., Nos. 2, 3, 4, 10, 12.

Roxbury. Dillaway, C. K. A history of the grammar school, or, "The Free Schoole of 1645 in Roxburie," with biographical sketches of the ministers of the first church, and other trustees. Roxbury, 1860.

EDUCATIONAL HISTORIES

(*Arranged alphabetically by authors*)

Brown, Elmer E. The making of our middle schools. An account of the development of secondary education in the United States. New York, 1903.

Bush, George Gary. History of higher education in Massachusetts. U. S. Bureau of Educ., Circ. of Information, No. 6, 1891.

Carter, James Gordon. The schools of Massachusetts in 1824. Old South Leaflets, No. 135. Boston.

Clews, Elsie W. Educational legislation and administration of the colonial governments. (Columbia Univ. Contrib. to Philos., Psychol., and Educ.) New York, 1899.

Edson, A. W. Supervision of schools in Massachusetts, including a history of its growth. . . . Boston, 1895.

Martin, George H. The evolution of the Massachusetts public school system. A historical sketch. New York, 1894.

Mowry, William A. Powers and duties of the school superintendents. Educational Review, ix., 38.

Pickard, J. L. School supervision. New York, 1890.

Prince, John T. The evolution of school supervision. Educational Review, xxii., 148.

Prince, John T. Report upon city and town supervision of schools. Sixty-third Report of the Mass. Board of Education. Chap. vii., p. 289.

TOWN HISTORIES.

(*Arranged alphabetically by towns*)

Boston . . . Winsor, Justin (editor). The memorial history of Boston, including Suffolk County, Mass. 1630–1880. 4 vols. Boston, 1880–1881.

Boston. History of Boston, from 1630 to 1856. Illust. Boston, 1856.

Cambridge. Paige, Lucius R. History of Cambridge, Mass. 1630–1877. . . . Boston, 1877.

Dedham. Worthington, Erastus. History of Dedham from the beginning of its settlement. . . . Boston, 1827.

Deerfield. Sheldon, George. History of Deerfield. . . . 2 vols. Deerfield, 1895–1896.

Douglas. Emerson, Wm. A. History of the town of Douglas. . . . Boston, 1879.

Dover. Smith, Frank. History of Dover. . . . Dover, 1897.

Eastham, Wellfleet, and Orleans. Pratt, Enoch. A comprehensive history, ecclesiastical and civil, of Eastham, Wellfleet, and Orleans. . . . Yarmouth, 1844.

Grafton. Pierce, Frederick Clifton. History of Grafton. . . . Worcester, 1879.

Hadley. Judd, Sylvester. History of Hadley, including the early history of Hatfield, South Hadley, Amherst, and Granby. Northampton, 1863.

Hanover. Barry, John S. Historical sketch of the town of Hanover. . . . Boston, 1853.

Lancaster. Marvin, Abijah P. History of the town of Lancaster. . . Lancaster, 1879.

Marlborough. Hudson, Charles. History of the town of Marlborough. . . . Boston, 1862.

Newbury. Coffin, Joshua. Sketch of the history of Newbury, Newburyport, and West Newbury, from 1635 to 1845. Boston, 1845.

Northampton. Trumbull, James Russell. History of Northampton. . . . 2 vols. Northampton, 1898.

North Bridgewater. Kingman, Bradford. History of North Bridgewater. Boston, 1866.

North Brookfield. Temple, J. H. History of North Brookfield. . . . North Brookfield, 1887.

Northfield. Sheldon, George, and Temple, J. H. History of the town of Northfield. . . . Albany, 1875.

Oxford. Daniels, George F. History of the town of Oxford. . . . Oxford, 1892.

Palmer. Temple, J. H. History of the town of Palmer. . . . Palmer, 1889.

Roxbury. Ellis, Charles M. History of Roxbury town. Boston, 1847.

Salem. Felt, Joseph B. Annals of Salem. 2 vols. 2d ed. Salem, 1845.

Springfield. Green, Mason A. Springfield. 1636–1886. History of town and city. . . . Springfield, 1888.

Sutton. Benedict, Wm. A., and Tracy, Hiram A. History of the town of Sutton. . . . Worcester, 1878.

Wenham. Allen, Myron O. History of Wenham. . . . Boston, 1860.

Whately. Temple, J. H. History of the town of Whately. . . . Boston, 1872.

Woburn. Sewall, Samuel. History of Woburn. . . . Boston, 1868.

OTHER HISTORIES

(*Arranged alphabetically by authors*)

Andrews, Charles McLean. Colonial self-government, 1652–1689. (The American Nation, vol. v.) New York, 1904.

Eggleston, Edward. The transit of civilization; from England to America in the seventeenth century. New York, 1901.

Osgood, Herbert L. The American colonies in the Seventeenth Century. 2 vols. New York, 1904.

Palfrey, John Gorham. Compendious history of New England. . . . 4 vols. Boston (1883).

Webster, William Clarence. Recent centralizing tendencies in state administration. New York, 1897.

Weeden, William Babcock. Economic and social history of New England. 1620–1789. 2 vols. Boston, 1894.

Whitten, Robert Harvey. Public administration in Massachusetts. The relation of central to local activity. New York, 1896–7.

Winthrop, John. History of New England, 1630–1649. 2 vols. Boston, 1853.